THE
WICCANING

THE
WICCANING

*A Step-by-Step Guide
to Becoming
a Modern Witch*

SISTER MOON

CITADEL PRESS
KENSINGTON PUBLISHING CORP.
www.kensingtonbooks.com

CITADEL PRESS books are published by

Kensington Publishing Corp.
850 Third Avenue
New York, NY 10022

Copyright © 2001 Sister Moon

All Kensington titles, imprints, and distributed lines are available at special quantity discounts for bulk purchases for sales promotions, premiums, fund raising, educational, or institutional use. Special book excerpts or customized printings can also be created to fit specific needs. For details, write or phone the office of the Kensington special sales manager: Kensington Publishing Corp., 850 Third Avenue, New York, NY 10022, attn: Special Sales Department, phone 1-800-221-2647.

Citadel Press logo Reg. U.S. Patent and Trademark Office
Citadel Press is a trademark of Kensington Publishing Corp.

First printing: February, 2001

10 9 8 7 6 5 4 3 2 1

Printed in the United States of America

Library of Congress Cataloging-in-Publication Data

Moon, Sister.
    The wiccaning : a step-by-step guide to becoming a modern witch / Sister Moon.
        p. cm.
    "A Citadel Press book."
    ISBN 0-8065-2128-7 (pbk.)
    1. Witchcraft.   2. Neopaganism.   3. Magic.   I. Title.
BF1571.M66 1999
133.4'3—dc21   99–32363
                                                                        CIP

To my Father,
my knight in shining armor,
and in loving memory
of my Mother and Grandmother

C⊕NTENTS

WHICH WENCH IS WITCH?

Observe the Wench that hums a tune,
And is nowhere to be found under rounded moon.
Look into the eyes for centers wide and pitch,
But do not question if thou be a Witch!
Her secrets are treasures, her tongue does not wag,
She has wisdom of old, but does not brag.
She dances with cats and laughs at the wind,
Her candles burn papers, but her hands never singe.
Her garments are black and she is adorned with jewels,
She heals the sick with her collection of tools.
Her garden will flourish with herbs and snakes,
She will steal your mind if you eat what she bakes.
Be forewarned, if thou kisses her lips,
For thou will be caught in the web that she knit.
She is scarred by the devil and never speaks lies,
She fears her heritage, so she claims a disguise.
Her scorn is like daggers burning the flesh,
To cheat her once will cause sudden death.
If all of these clues seem to weary the mind,
There is one more if thou be so blind.
Her hands are worn, but her thumbs are twist,
Then be thou certain, this Wench is a Witch!

PREFACE

I know who you are. You're the person who can't help but get excited when hearing Celtic music. You're the person who doesn't fit into the mold of organized religion. And you're the person who feels transfixed by the light of the full moon. I know who you are and you're not alone.

Sometimes our past life memories seep into our present lives. When touching certain magickal stones, I recall a vision of a different lifetime. When casting a love spell, I see the face of a man I have never met. I find myself searching for familiarity in all paths. Practicing Wicca is like going home again.

My maternal Grandmother was my teacher for Wicca. From reading tarot cards to casting healings, her knowledge of the religion was my tutelage. Though my Grandmother was not a well-educated person, her knowledge of the craft and applied wisdom presented a wonderful opportunity for my sister and me. Her purity of heart was a constant reminder in our lives. Her arthritic hands sketched an illustration to help us understand. She drew three hearts. The first heart was colored solid black. The second heart was torn in half, one part black and the other white. The third heart was very white and shiny. She said the first heart was for people who are self-absorbed, people who only care about themselves. The second heart represented the majority of people in today's world. They care for themselves, but help others once in a while to experience good feelings or even to benefit themselves later in some way. The third heart belonged to a true Witch. The pure heart represented people who help everyone, including themselves, without expecting gratitude or glory, and without harming anyone or anything.

Do the following statements ring true for you? Are they compatible with your personal belief system?

1. There is a Supreme Source of power in the universe. This Source has both female and male energy.
2. You desire to connect to the Supreme Source of power.
3. There is a balance to everything.
4. As mortals, we possess concentrated energy that we have not yet tapped into.
5. Nothing is coincidental.
6. You desire to improve the Earth and all its inhabitants.
7. You are searching for wholeness and perfection.
8. Everything is a combination of female and male energies within our own bodies and lives.
9. You would like to celebrate our natural changes.
10. You are driven by the continual search for truth in all matters.

If the concepts in these statements are agreeable to you, then Wicca may be your path. This book is designed to give you guidelines, not to walk the path for you. We all retain the privilege of free will, a mind to think with, and a heart to feel with. If you do not agree with a concept, then search for the truth behind that concept and accept nothing less. Wicca may be a path, but the journey is all yours.

So Mote It Be.

ACKNΘWLEDGⅢENTS

To Belladonna, for the beautiful openings she wrote for each chapter. I also wish to thank Lorin Dobberstine for the wonderful artwork she contributed. To Pam Mencher, who forced me to finish this book. To all of my Wiccan students who kept the inspiration at all times. To Sherry Fobes and the Friday nights she contributed and for little Mojo, too. To my children, who painfully understood why Mommy was busy. To Robert K. Berkel for being a minor genius. And a most gracious thank-you to Diane Davis, who worked as hard as I did to produce this book and who also sacrificed all ten of her toes in the process.

THE
WICCANING

I

THE SIMPLE TRUTH

Reflect thy image into mirrors of past,
To gaze upon Witches and spells they've cast.
Slip thy feet into pagan shoes,
Walk the pathway of simple truths.
Be yet chosen a Wiccan child,
The world forewarned would be too wild.
Unleash the spirit and open the eyes,
To dance among the Wiccan wise.

BELLADONNA

Defining Wicca

Witchcraft is not a hobby or an occasional fling of magick. It is a religion—an ancient religion that predates Jesus Christ. Wicca is the proper name for the religion of Witchcraft. The word *wicca* literally means *the wise one*. The practice of Witchcraft is the practice of wisdom.

Wicca is a pagan religion, meaning it is outside of Christianity, Judaism, and Islam. The word *neopagan* represents a more modern paganism. The Christian religion is based upon the Bible and the teachings of Jesus Christ. Judaism is based upon the Old Testament of the Bible and its interpretation through the Talmud. Islam is based upon the worship of Allah, and Mohammed is his prophet.

Before Judaism, Christianity, and Islam became organized religions, there were only pagans. Prior to the advent of these religions, paganism was highly respected. Witches were revered for their knowledge and their ability to heal and divine. Royalty often consulted with Witches.

Wiccans acknowledge that Judaism, Christianity, and Islam have structure and foundation, but Wiccans believe that two supreme deities govern all. These deities are the Goddess and the God. It is believed that these two powers cocreated the universe and Their presence is within all of us.

Wiccans in general do not agree with or deny the teachings of Jesus Christ. Opinions about Christianity are considered to be a personal choice in the heart of each individual Witch. The majority of Wiccans do not believe in a heaven or hell, nor do they believe in the lower deity of the Devil, Satan, or Lucifer. Each Witch can differ from these beliefs as long as he or she believes in the worship of the Goddess and the God. Like other religions, Wicca has a basic infrastructure, but each Wiccan can differ on these three points: the existence of heaven, hell, or the Devil.

Wicca is an earth religion. We believe in harnessing energy the universe supplies and infusing it into magick. This entails the use of candles, herbs, and incenses, in conjunction with prayer, visualization, meditation, and spells.

History

Throughout history, we have witnessed the slaughter of innocent people because of their religious preferences. We have seen Christians, Jews, and many others persecuted for their beliefs.

However, most people who were accused of being Witches were not witches. Maybe a handful of the slaughtered ones were pagans, but not even one percent were actual Witches. All of these deaths were in vain. At least, the Christian and Jewish martyrs admitted their religious preferences, whereas the accused Witches strongly protested that Witchcraft was not their religion, but they were persecuted anyway. So why the dreadful fear of Witchery? Power. People are afraid of someone having power over their lives. Yet witchcraft is not a religion based on power, nor does it try to seize control over other people. It is simply the loving worship of the Goddess and the God.

The ancient Greeks and Romans believed the Wiccans were capable of many different things. They believed they had supernatural powers that could be used in many ways. The public didn't believe all Witches were evil, but that Witches had power and that belief was dangerous enough. It would be pointless to say Witches are powerless because no one is powerless. We all retain the power of free will and absolutely no one person can take that from you unless you give it to them.

The thing most dreaded among the Greeks and Romans during this period was the threat of the *evil eye*. They accused only the Wiccans of having this power. The evil eye is an intense look or stare. It is meant for one purpose: a warning. The warning is of forbearance, to refrain from an action. Yes, the evil eye still exists! The Greeks and Romans gave the evil eye much more credit than it actually deserves. They believed it was the reason for plague, drought, famine, earthquakes, and so forth. Any natural or unnatural catastrophe was blamed on the evil eye. This is where the expression "if looks could kill" came from.

The evil eye has no real power, it is simply a warning, but the Wiccans do take pride in their evil eye. If you think about it, though, every mother in the world has the evil eye. Visualize a child reaching for a cookie right before dinnertime. The child sees his mother watching him and is frozen, motionless with fear. The child puts down the cookie and walks away. The mother has the best evil eye going and no one accuses her of being evil. In Italy, if a man were scorned by any pagan female, he would grab his genitals and fall to the ground in a seizurelike manner, screaming, "Evil eye!" I can only assume he was afraid his genitals would fall off. He would then run to the nearest Witch to unhex him. It is significant to note that he did not run to the nearest church or government official for help, but rather to a Witch. The Witch would then remove the hex with a spell and instantly the man would be cured. This was easily possible since, first of all, the evil eye is not a curse; it is simply a warning. Second, if a curse were to be placed upon someone, it would not be by a Witch. Witches, however, can remove curses. The average Witch of ancient times probably snickered as the man and his fear left her home after she removed the hex.

During the Inquisition, the Catholic Church and government officials began an organized campaign to root out all "heretics." Pagan religions were deemed devil worship. Wiccans, in particular, were stunned by this. They didn't even believe in the devil and now they were accused of worshiping him? At this time in history, the members of the Catholic Church and the government outnumbered Wiccans by more than a hundred to one. The Witches went into hiding.

The penalty for paganism was severe, to say the least. Most of the people were humiliated and then slaughtered. The methods of execution were not humane, either. The tortures these people endured are beyond comprehension.

Over the span of 400 years, millions of innocent people in Europe alone were executed in the name of heresy. The Church and the government were united and omnipotent. Personal grudges and money issues often drove jealous officials to select the so-called heretics.

Wiccans survived throughout this time, but they covered their identities carefully. The accusations decreased slightly over the years until another Witch hunt broke out in America. The year was 1692. The European law against pagans was still in effect, so no one professed any belief other than Christianity. During one year, a minimum of 141 people were imprisoned in Salem, Massachusetts, on charges of Witchery. Only one of those was actually a pagan. Ironically, this real pagan survived the mania while the innocent ones were slaughtered and imprisoned.

More Recent History

In 1951, the law in England was rewritten because of a Wiccan High Priest named Gerald B. Gardner. While employed as a civil servant, he decided to come out of the closet with his religious preference—Witchcraft. He demonstrated a ritual to the Parliament and explained the nature of his worship so they could see that this religion was not about demons, destruction, sacrifice, or ungodliness. Wicca was portrayed in its true form: the worship of the Goddess and the God. The Parliament declared Witchcraft a legal religion. In 1953, Gerald B. Gardner petitioned his right to coven, and that right was also declared legal.

The majority of covens are still underground because the world may still not accept Witches. It is easier to perpetuate a negative label than to accept a tolerant view.

Four Types of Witches

There are four basic organizations of Wiccans:

Hereditarians   People practicing the oldest of Wiccan traditions. This is the cult that has passed down spells and information from generation to generation. It has been alive for thousands of years. It is a quiet sect that until recently told no one outside the Wiccan tradition of its beliefs. Now this religion is open to those who wish to study, learn, and live by these beliefs. The teachings of this book are based on this tradition.

Traditionals   Practitioners of beliefs based upon historic rituals that originated in Europe.

Gardnerians   People belonging to a sect based upon the beliefs and rituals of a High Priest named Gerald B. Gardner, an English Witch who was successfully published. He died in 1964.

Alexandrians   People who follow the teachings of a modern English Witch who devised specific ceremonies and rituals.

Three Colors of Witches

There are three types of Witches:

The Gray Witch   A Wiccan novice is a Gray Witch. This person studies the religion for no less than one year and one day with the intention of becoming a White Witch. The Gray Witch does not have full control of magickal abilities until after her initiation. Also, Gray Witches can be called upon by a White Witch to aid in ritual work and they must comply.

The White Witch   The White Witch is an experienced sorceress of white magick. In order to achieve this position, one must be able to pass initiation and live life by all ten rules. This position lasts a lifetime as long as the Witch continues the commitment to the Wiccan religion.

The Black Witch   Black Witches are not associated with either Gray or White Witches, or even the Wiccan religion. This is usually due to their affiliation with Satan or other dark forces. Their beliefs are almost completely opposite the Wiccan rules. The vast majority of the public believes all Witches are the same. Due to this misconception, most Wiccans are still underground and the public only hears about the Black, or evil, Witches.

Female Wiccans are called Witches and male Wiccans are also called Witches. However, some male Witches prefer to identify themselves as Warlocks, due to the more masculine tone. Each individual coven votes on the word to be used for male Witches. Every Witch also has a secret name known only among the coven and other Witches. Each coven has a secret name as well, to identify itself to other covens. It is important to choose your Wiccan name carefully and to make your name magickal.

The coven is the gathering of Witches for the specific purpose of a unison ritual work of magick. Covens are extremely secret and the location where the coven meets is called the covenstead. Only the members of the coven know who is in the coven, the Wiccan name of each member, and the location where the coven is held. Some covens rotate covensteads for security purposes. The contents of the covens are absolutely secret. Once a coven is formed, no outsiders will have any knowledge of what occurs therein. This is the oath of the coven.

When Gray Witches pass the initiation to White Witch, the next step is to practice Wicca for a minimum of one year. After that time, they can study to further their spiritual growth and to become High Priestess or High Priest, or can simply remain White Witches to study and practice Wicca.

The average age of a High Priestess or Priest is thirty-six years old. Once a person proceeds from Gray to White Witch, this person can retain the position of White Witch for an eternity or move up the hierarchy as his or her experience and knowledge develops. The High Priestess or Priest is not only a practitioner of the craft, but is also a teacher to Gray Witches. This position usually falls to the leader of the coven. It is not uncommon for covens to have numerous High Priestesses or Priests within their circle, but only one is the acting leader.

The highest level within the coven is the Crone. Most people imagine the Crone as a wicked old Witch, but actually a Crone is simply an experienced, sometimes elderly, woman.

There is a saying, "Never teach magick to the untrained because they will end up burning themselves, as well as others." Magick is serious business. There is no *undo*; once a spell has been cast, it is done. The responsibility lies with the High Priestess or Priest to teach this crucial lesson correctly.

Three Times Three

The law of three times three means that whatever a Witch puts out magickally will come back threefold. Special care must be taken to ensure that only positive energies are returned to the practitioner. This is based on the concept of karma: What goes around, comes around.

In the Hereditarian belief, we honor the Triple Goddess and the Triple God. The Triple Goddess is the Maiden, the Mother, and the Crone. The Triple God is the Father, the Son, and the Holy Spirit.

The God is known as the Horned God or the God of the Hunt. Because the pictorial image of a man with horns is associated with the devil, the general public assumes the God is a demon. The God worshiped by Witches does not have hooves for his hands or feet. This would once again associate the God with the devil. Modern Witches visualize the God without the horns and just in the image of a beautiful male. The God is also known as the God of the Sun.

Some Wiccans believe in the worship of lower goddesses and gods corresponding to the mythological era. Some also feel that the Goddess is superior to the God. In the Hereditarian belief, we feel They are equals, and no lower goddesses or gods exist.

The Origin of the Goddess and the God

In the beginning there was the Goddess. She was supreme and nurturing in all that was. The Goddess, being divine, created the Earth. She carpeted the Earth in the velvet of green grass, a sign of eternity. She planted trees that bore fruit, a sign of her fertility. She was pleased.

As time went on, the Goddess sat alone in the heavens. Her only companion in the heavens was the Moon. Her only companion below her was the Earth. The Goddess became lonely. As a result of her loneliness, the Goddess cried tears of salt and water. The tears pooled together on Earth and became oceans.

To cure herself of her loneliness, the Goddess impregnated herself with a seed. The seed was a life force. For ten full moons, the Goddess carried the seed within herself. She gave birth to a Son. Her Son gave the Goddess so much warmth that she created a heavenly symbol of her warmth and happiness; thus, she placed the Sun in the sky.

The Son of the Goddess grew from seed to Boy-God and then to God. The Goddess was very pleased.

With the seed of the God, the Goddess became fertile once again.

The Goddess carried the seed for another ten moons. The God became weak and started his dying process. As the Sun grew weaker, so did the God. The hours of daylight weakened. The Earth became cold and the God died.

The Goddess gave birth to the Son. It was not another Son, but the same Son. The Goddess nurtured the Son from seed, to Boy-God and then again to God.

As a sign of the eternal process of life, the Goddess created the seasons: A time for seeding. A time for growing. A time for harvesting. A time for dying.

The Goddess was pleased with her eternal cycle of life. For every year that passes, the Goddess places a new star in the heavens as a sign of Her happiness.

This is not a belief in incest, but rather of the Divine Goddess and God and the seasons of nature.

More to Learn

The idea behind magick and performing spells is to harness the energy from the earth and transform it into reality. Not one ounce of magick is granted without the approval of the Goddess and God. A Witch can have a magickal cupboard filled with every herb, incense, candle, and oil known to mankind, but if the Witch cannot abide by the Wiccan laws or obtain approval from the Goddess and God, then no magick can occur.

There are several practices a Witch needs to learn: the art of divining, spirit communications, spell casting, healings, and clearings. Each will be covered in depth in later chapters.

There are eight holy days, or Sabbats. Celebrating the Sabbats is an age-old tradition that has survived for centuries. Esbats are ritual gatherings under the full moon. There are twelve to thirteen per year. Witches are highly festive people, but rituals are performed before any festivities begin.

A special book is necessary to record your magickal information. This book can be called either a Grimoire or a Book of Shadows. The Grimoire can be any color or design on the cover and the pages can be either lined or unlined. The Book of Shadows must have solid black covers and unlined white paper. In these books, the Witch records all kinds of charts, magickal tables, herbs, oils, incenses, and, of course, spells. All information must be handwritten by the owner. These books take years of work to complete and are a priceless collection to the Witch. Each book is private, never to be revealed to an outsider—ever! The purpose of this book is not to educate curiosity seekers. When the book is completely finished, the Witch must write a spell on both of the inside covers. These spells are designed to protect your book from prying eyes. My grandmother used to refer to it as "cursing the works." This is simply an arrangement of rhyming words intended to scare anyone who picks up your book. I have lost several of my Grimoires and had them quite promptly returned after the person read the covers. It's kind of an insurance policy.

The Way It Is

The Wiccan religion is a non-proselytizing religion. This means there are no recruiters, door knockers, or evangelical witnesses to sway you to come over to our religion. No true Wiccans would ever try to convince or convert another person. We do not care what religion you are as long as you leave ours alone. Wiccans believe there is truth in all religions. Whatever religion you truly believe in is what we want you to practice. By the same token, do not try to convince us that yours is better. Witches realize that all people are on different paths to enlightenment. Some people feel the need to suffer for their beliefs. Others want to sway the world to go to their church. There are many different paths to the Goddess and God, and absolutely no one should be denied the journey. Not everyone marches to the beat of one drummer. As a matter of fact, nine out of ten Witches prefer dancing to marching.

Odds and Ends

The expression "So Mote It Be," is said at the closing of every incantation and ritual work. The words literally mean "It must be." Incantations are the arrangement of magickal words that invokes the spiritual aids and reveals the intent of the spell. Frequently, incantations rhyme like poetry. All magick has a rhythm.

The difference between the two words *magic* and *magick* is the performer. A magician like David Copperfield uses illusions to perform magic tricks. A Witch, with the blessing of the Goddess and God, uses magick to benefit everyone.

Purity of Heart

The wisdom of Solomon is what a Witch needs to learn and practice every day. The seven laws of magick (Balance, Maturity, Compassion, Wisdom, Self-Discipline, Perseverance, and Devotion), the Wiccan Rede (Harm ye none, then do as ye will), the one Truism (complete worship of the Goddess and the God), and purity of heart encompass the entire focus of a Witch and are the ten rules a Witch abides by.

Let's put down some guidelines about what a Witch is allowed and not allowed to do. Is it ethical to cast a love spell on someone? Get the facts first. Is the person you want to bewitch married? If so, the answer is no; get over it. What if the person is engaged or in a relationship with someone else? As long as the person is not married, the field is open for magick. Remember, you cannot break people's free will if they do not want it broken. Is it ethical to cast money spells, employment spells, healing spells, attraction spells, sex spells, protection spells, and so forth, on others? Ask yourself these questions:

If I do this spell, will anyone get hurt?
Am I being selfish and not considering what the outcome may be?
What will be the consequences of this spell?
Do I really need this?
Remember, always use magick as a last resort.

You are able to do any of these types of spells as long as it is for the right reasons. Be careful of what you are asking for because, chances are, you're going to get it.

The dreaded subject of enemies always pops in here. For whatever reason, all of us have some enemies whether we acknowledge that fact or not. Are you allowed to hurt your enemies or cause them any harm? The answer is no. What if someone is attacking you with slander or even physically? You are then permitted to bind them. This is a magickal way of forcing them to cease the attack. The binding is a simple restraint. A Witch is also permitted to return someone's negative energy back to the sender. Purity of heart is an absolute when dealing with enemies or when doing any kind of magick.

Before any person can decide if this religion is right for him or her, there must be a conscious decision made. Can this person abide by all ten rules? A pure-hearted person does not do a kind deed for someone with the thought of gaining a reward. A person with a pure heart practices kindness on a daily basis for the simple purpose of helping someone. If you are selecting this path for self-empowerment, then this is not the religion for you. This religion is based upon worship of the Goddess and the God. The only power here is within Them.

THE TEN BASICS

2

To gaze inside a Witch's heart,
Glowing white and never dark.
Upon the shine there must read,
Ten rules of life that must be heed.
An Harm Ye None is how it's told,
To start one on the Wiccan road.
Perseverance and Wisdom is the fashion,
Blended together with Compassion.
Worship the Goddess and God that be,
Self-discipline, Balance, and Maturity.
Purity of Heart and then Devotion,
Sanction the path in deosil motion.
Follow the ten and not one less,
If a Witch is what you Profess.
Ten rules for the wise and fools be daft,
To unlock the magick of the craft.

BELLADONNA

The Doctrine

There are ten basic rules to the Wiccan religion that must be abided by at all times. If even one rule is broken or deleted, no magick will occur. By following these rules you will not only be an awesome Witch, but you will become a better person. These rules are broken down into Seven Laws of Magick, one Rede, one Truism, and one basic Principle.

The Seven Laws of Magick are:

1. Balance
2. Maturity
3. Compassion
4. Wisdom
5. Self-Discipline
6. Perseverance
7. Devotion

One Rede   "An harm ye none, then do as ye will."
One Truism   The complete worship of the Goddess and the God.
One Principle   Purity of heart.

Balance

Patsy is a woman in her seventies. She is highly prioritized and balanced. I often marvel at her wisdom in child-rearing. She independently raised six successful children and has better than a dozen grandchildren and great grandchildren. Patsy has a beautiful, but determined soul. She told me she never had to raise her hand or her voice to any of her children. As I unhandcuffed my oldest daughter from a kitchen chair, I asked her how she did it. She shared the secret of honesty, balance, and unconditional love. I asked for a definition of balance and she said, "calmness, priority, and understanding."

To be balanced means

1. To prioritize and not become obsessive.
2. To be stable and symmetrical in your ways of thinking and behaving.
3. To know that other people do not always share your values.

Maturity

Diana is a Crone in a new body. She stands slightly taller than five feet, but her aura is ten feet above that. I always jest that she is larger than life. She often reminds me that observing other people will always uncover personal revelations. She gave me the example of a young paraplegic man on whom she does healing work, and shared his progress with me. I asked her how he endures life without giving in to an overwhelming sense of self-pity. She responded with her secret to defusing explosive and destructive attitudes of "woe is me." The answer is maturity.

To be mature means:

1. To accept life and to be responsible for your own actions and thoughts.
2. To be centered with harmonious energy.
3. To develop, search, and grow in only positive light.

Compassion

My third grade teacher back in the mid-1960s was radiant with love. I was one of many children who had an obvious physical affliction and was teased unmercifully by the other children. Even though her compassion was enormous, she made me realize our bodies are merely shells for the inner person, and it is this inner person who really matters. I learned that being different puts one in the major-ity rather than the minority. She believed in emphasizing positive attributes in order to diminish the negative ones. Instead of letting me hide within my shell, she encouraged me to believe I was special in other ways. For the brief period of one school year I felt accepted and loved because she believed in not hiding the truth, but rather in lifting it up.

To have compassion means

1. To empathize with others.

2. To be charitable.

3. To not overwhelm but rather enhance with kindness.

Wisdom

Bud is a father and a grandfather. He wears a Robert Redford smile that is always captivating. Bud refers to wisdom as coming from a fictitious elder called the Old Wise One. No matter how sour or bleak a situation, Bud always comes through with a few words from the Old Wise One that seem to relieve the tension and pain. "A dose of laughter will harmonize a discontented heart," he would say. Oddly enough, his words of humor always chime with truth. I asked him once if he ever planned to record his wise tidbits. He just squinted his blue eyes and said, "No, I think Confucius might feel threatened."

To have wisdom means:

1. To have insight and foresight into situations.

2. To use discretion, good judgment, and sensitivity.

3. To have perception, prudence, and humility.

Self-Discipline

Pam is my health guru. For any ailment on this planet, she has a cure. She is constantly brewing up herbs, potions, and so forth to heal people, animals, and the earth. She is a devout vegetarian and a strong activist for animal rights. Her mind is brilliant and her humor is candid and disarming. The oddity about Pam is her affliction with dyslexia. She sees most words and numbers in reverse. I refer to her as a Witch with a twist. Because of her dyslexia, she has to repeat her work two or three times to verify she has done it correctly. Pam has mastered intense levels of concentration and her work performance is completely perfect due to her self-discipline skills.

To have self-discipline means

1. To have complete control of the self at all times.
2. To have focus, concentration, and patience.
3. To behave with integrity.

Perseverance

Diola is a driven woman who works fourteen-hour days, five to six days a week. It isn't her work that drives her, but the few hours she strives to have each day to read. The knowledge she is craving is "perfection of the spirit." I believe she has an old soul and it is trying to gain levels of Angel-like existence, or even Master Guide levels for the time when she passes from this earth. Her purity and compassion rival her infectious smile. There is no doubt in my mind that she will obtain all she needs to know before she leaves this plane. In the meantime, she happily propels forward.

To have perseverance means

1. To have a positive attitude and positive mental drive.
2. To have steadfastness and endurance.
3. To exercise tenacity, patience, and determination.

Devotion

Terra is a gifted genius whom most people view as the Zany Cat Lady. One day she came across an abandoned restaurant housing about two dozen feral cats. She contacted many organizations to see if anyone would rescue these animals, but to no avail. The end result would be extermination since they were feral. She felt she could not only rescue these animals, but actually tame them so that she could find good homes for each of them. Due to her compassion, determination, and devotion, each cat has been tamed and restored to perfect health.

To have devotion means

1. To have honor and dedication in all you do.
2. To make commitments resulting in positive change.
3. To conduct yourself with reverence and selflessness.

Harm Ye None

Lorin is an Indian of the Cherokee tribe. She is a lovely and mysterious woman. Her life has never been easy yet her attitude is always very optimistic. I have known her for over ten years and have never heard an unkind word come from her mouth. I witnessed a woman who became jealous and obsessed with Lorin and tried to destroy her. I performed a binding with Lorin to protect her and keep this woman at bay. It would have been so easy to turn hateful and resentful of this enemy, but instead Lorin included a special prayer of healing for this woman's soul so she would not be jealous any longer.

To harm ye none means

1. To erase all ego, hate, and discrimination.
2. To not harm, damage, or impair anyone for self-gain or vengeance.
3. To cast magick benefiting all and destroying none.

Worship of the Goddess and God

Carrie is a beautiful woman who has never missed a day of church or prayer. She has developed a one-on-one relationship with the Universal Powers. Not a day goes by when someone does not call Carrie and ask to put a name on her prayer list. She lives in the Denver, Colorado, area where the weather is unpredictable and can be spontaneously severe, but nothing deters Carrie from her daily regime of reverence. As sure as the sun rises each morning, Carrie will continue her worship rituals.

To worship the Goddess and God means

1. To honor and respect Them and to respect your life, body, mind, heart, and soul, as They have given these to you. You are a direct creation of Their love.
2. To glorify Them, not yourself.
3. To regard the Deities in every decision you make.

Purity of Heart

Zari is from Iran. She has been in America for several years and has built a successful business doing healing work. She has adopted the ways of her new country well, yet has not renounced who she is. Her gentle spirit is breathtaking. While maintaining a full-time job, Zari studied for one year to become a Witch, and her enthusiasm never waned. Numerous adjectives describe purity of heart, but none of them compares to experiencing Zari. The purest heart makes a conscious choice to live in love. The best description I can offer you about Zari is, she has the soul of an Angel.

To have purity of heart means

1. To be free of all negativity.
2. To give and receive unconditional love.
3. To release all selfishness and be filled with the spirit of the Goddess and God.

GETTING STARTED

As the spider weaves the web,
The Witch will sew with silken thread.
Taught by nature and Crones of past,
Invoke the Corners for the cast.
Cleanse the tools for the altar,
Practice perfection to avoid falter.
Adorn the body in Wiccan attire,
To raise the energy even higher.
Light the way for the Gray to learn,
Covet the cauldron for wishes to burn.
Open the book and strum the harp,
For this is where all Witches start.

BELLADONNA

Tools of the trade

There are ten basic tools necessary for setting an altar to do magick. The altar is a clean, flat surface that is the center and focus of a magick circle. The altar is the place where all magick begins. The tools needed are:

1. One large white candle. This is called the Unity candle. Its purpose is to represent the union of power. It is placed in the very center of the altar.

2. One white candle. This candle is called the Goddess candle. It is placed to the right of the Unity candle and its function is to represent the power of the Goddess.

3. One white candle. This candle is called the God candle. It is placed to the left of the Unity candle and its function is to represent the power of the God.

4. A small container of salt. The preference is sea salt, but any salt will do. This is to create the holy water of consecration. It is placed directly before the God candle.

5. A small dish of clean water. This is to mix with the salt to create the holy water of consecration. The dish is placed directly before the Goddess candle.

6. A pentagram. The pentagram is a five-pointed star, which is the Wiccan symbol. Its five points represent Earth, Air, Fire, Water, and Spirit. It is placed directly in front of the Unity candle.

THE ALTAR

God Candle   Unity Candle   Goddess
                                     Candle

Ritual Salt   Pentagram   Holy Water

Athame   Incense Burner   Chalice

Cauldron

7. An incense burner. The incense burner is used for burning incense, which attracts the powers of heaven and earth to aid in whatever spell or ritual you are casting. The position of the incense burner is directly before the Pentagram.

8. An athame. The athame is a dull sword or small knife. Its purpose is to channel the energy in a ritual or it is simply used to call the Quadrants. It is placed near the salt container.

9. A chalice. The chalice is a ceremonial cup. Its purpose is to hold the liquid contents that may be used in any spell or ritual. It is placed near the dish of water.

10. A cauldron. The cauldron is a cast-iron pot. Its purpose is to hold the contents of things that may be burned in a ritual or spell. It is also the symbol of ancient Wiccan art. It is placed in the center in front of the incense burner.

It may help to remember that the altar is divided into three sections: the Unity placement, the Goddess placement, and the God placement. The items that fall under the Unity placement are: the Unity candle, the pentagram, the incense burner, and the cauldron. The Goddess items are: the Goddess candle, the chalice, and the dish of water. The God items are: the God candle, the salt container, and the athame.

Casting a Circle

The first spell that a Gray Witch learns is how to cast a magickal circle. A magick circle is a sacred space of learning and worship. Prepare and set your altar before you begin.

It will be necessary to cast a circle for every ritual ever performed. This casting is called the Call of Order. The middle part of the ceremony is designed for whatever spells or rituals you are doing. The final phase is called Opening the Circle and takes place after the rituals are completed and it is time to release the power from the circle.

THE TOWERS

EARTH	AIR	FIRE	WATER
"LAW"	"LIFE"	"LIGHT"	"LOVE"
Ruled by GODDESS	Ruled by GOD	Ruled by GOD	Ruled by GODDESS
Guarded by URIEL	Guarded by RAPHAEL	Guarded by MICHAEL	Guarded by GABRIEL
Circle Tool PENTACLE	Circle Tool WAND	Circle Tool SWORD	Circle Tool CUP
WINTER	SPRING	SUMMER	AUTUMN
Quadrant NORTH	Quadrant EAST	Quadrant SOUTH	Quadrant WEST
Elemental Entities GNOMES	Elemental Entities SYLPHS	Elemental Entities SALAMANDERS	Elemental Entities UNDINES
Sun Emphasis MIDNIGHT	Sun Emphasis DAWN	Sun Emphasis NOONDAY	Sun Emphasis SUNSET

THE PENTAGRAM

Spirit

Air

Water

Earth

Fire

TO PROPEL WITH MOTION

Deosil (Gee sul)

Clockwise
(Starting from the center)

Widdershins

Counterclockwise
(Starting from the center)

The Call of Order

Light the Unity candle. Place three pinches of sea salt into the fresh water and say:

> *I cleanse thee, Spirit of Salt and Spirit of Water. I cast out all impurities that lie within thee. This is my will, So Mote It Be.*

Sprinkle the perimeter of the circle in a clockwise motion with the salt water and say:

> *Blessed be sunrise, sunset, midnight, and noon,*
> *When two or more shall gather to draw down the moon.*
> *So Mote It Be.*

If you are the only person present when casting this circle, just leave out the words as you are sprinkling the area.

Face the direction of East and, with the athame in hand, draw the sign of a pentagram in the air, starting at the top of the star. Then recite the invocation. For each direction, face the compass point, draw the pentagram, and recite the invocation.

> (Face East) *Raphael.*
> *I call upon the Power of the East.*
> *May the Air lift me so my mind will feast.*

> (Face South) *Michael.*
> *I call upon the Power of the South.*
> *May the Fire of free will never burn out.*

> (Face West) *Gabriel.*
> *I call upon the Power of the West.*
> *May the Water of emotion join my quest.*

> (Face North) *Uriel.*
> *I call upon the Power of the North.*
> *May the Earth be my body from this day forth.*
> *So Mote It Be.*

From the Unity candle, light the God candle on the left and then light the Goddess candle on the right and say:

PROPER MOTIONS FOR INVOCATION
AND BANISHMENT

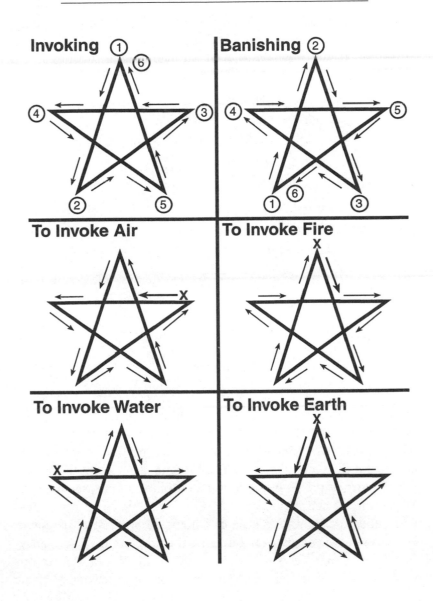

Invoking

Banishing

To Invoke Air

To Invoke Fire

To Invoke Water

To Invoke Earth

I call upon God, Creator of man. I welcome Thee to empower this
magick circle. I call upon the Goddess, Creator of woman. I
welcome Thee to empower this magick circle.

The circle is now cast. (This is when you would cast your spells.)

To open the circle: Face the direction of West and, with the
athame in hand, draw the sign of the pentagram, starting at the
bottom of the star and say:

To the North, South, East, and West.
With gratitude and praise, so be blessed.

Extinguish the God candle first, then the Goddess candle, and say:

To the mighty God and the Goddess that be,
With gratitude and praise, So Mote It Be.

Hold the Unity candle in your hands and recite the next verse before
extinguishing the candle:

This candle now shines of one.
Our journey has now begun.
This circle is now open.
But forever, unbroken.
So Mote It Be.

Wardrobe

During a High Sabbat, Wicca attire is required. Wiccans prefer clothing that is nonbinding. Traditional Wicca wardrobe consists of a
black ceremonial robe and also a gown of any solid color (black is
often chosen.) The cape is to be worn as a symbol of *blanketed protection* and the gown should be free-flowing. This is not to say that
pants, skirts, and blouses are not acceptable, because they are.
Maybe the Witches who live in Beverly Hills (are there any?) dress
with unity and more of a fashion statement. The rest of us down-
home types of Witches wear garments that are footloose and fancy-
free. During High Sabbats, the capes are always worn. The reasons
vary, from protecting people from the weather to having everyone

appear similar. At any rate, what is
in the heart of the Witch and not
what is on the back makes the big
difference in magick.

Please understand that clothing of
any kind is a total option. Some
Wiccans are skyclad, meaning without any clothing. When I perform
rituals by myself, this feels most natural to me. It is the only way to be
completely free and in total harmony
with the Goddess and God and all of
nature. When I am doing rituals with
my coven, we all wear clothes. This
is what we feel comfortable with.
Other covens may choose differently.

One point worth mentioning
about the Wicca wardrobe is that the
general public should not be able to
view it and say, "Oh, there goes a

Witch!" I have actually witnessed two people getting out of a car
during the day wearing black ceremonial robes, with their hoods
on and walking down a busy street to someone's house. There was
obviously some sort of coven meeting, but absolutely everyone
around knew about it. By the time six cars had arrived at that house,
the police showed up with flashing lights and sirens. All of the traf-
fic on the street stopped because people were either hiding in neigh-
boring houses, watching the spectacle, or hiding out in their cars in
fear of their pets being slaughtered by the Satanists. The police
stayed inside for about an hour before they left. What did this profit
the coven? Nothing. I would wager that the person's house was the
covenstead and it was now exposed. No one wants to be a neighbor
of scary-looking people. The average person associates black robes
with Satanists. Thus, the proud Witches who did not care what the
world thought of them had to find a new covenstead.

Please use discretion when dealing with the public. Always use discretion for the protection of yourself, your coven, and, most of all, your magick. Being proud of your religion and your association to Wicca should be evident by the contentment and harmony of your life. Neon signs are not advised and neither is being obviously different in clothing. Throughout history, when innocent people were accused and persecuted for being Witches, it was due to the fact that they looked a bit different. The real Witches were the ones who survived because they did not stand out among the crowd. When wearing your ceremonial or Wiccan wardrobe, wear it with pride, but wear it so that people outside of the religion cannot detect you.

The Cord of Measure, also known as the cingula, is a rope-type belt that is made and worn on the outside of the gown. The Cord of Measure should be made to be your exact height plus one inch. The colors of the Cords will vary, depending on what level you have attained. The average practicing White Witch will have a cord that is either all black or a mixture of black and gold. The High Priestess will have a cord that is either all white or white and gold. The Crone will have a cord that is either purple or purple and gold. Very young novices (teenagers) who have not received their Wiccaning should make a Cord of Measure that has many colors and includes beads. The Witch should either make her own cord or have another Witch make it for her. If neither is available, most occult stores will have a Witch make one upon request. The Cord of Measure should be worn at all coven meetings.

C⊕L⊕R MAGICK

As the waxing moon calls to me,
A time for spells and colors weaved.
White to clense with purity,
Blue to protect like an ocean breeze.
Yellow to heal with the warming sun,
Pink for love till my days are done.
Red for passion to lift my soul,
Purple for power to reach my goals.
Green for abundance in deep dark wells,
Orange to bewitch all that I compel.
Light the night with colors ablaze,
Lift the magick with a smoky haze.
Dance and laugh with a voice that sings,
Fly with the Angels upon their wings.
Color the sky with rainbows bright,
Upon the broom that sweeps the night.

BELLADONNA

There is magick in colors! Every color has its very own vibration and magickal potential. By using color in spell casting, you have sent a very powerful message into the cosmos. When aligning colors for a magickal purpose, you have made harmony in the Universe. Color can make or break a spell. By using colors correctly, you can achieve the most positive results.

People, as well as animals, are greatly affected by colors. I watched an attorney prepare a witness for court and one of the first things he mentioned was "Don't wear green when you are on the witness stand." I could not believe my ears. I asked him the reason for this and he said that people who wear green are not as believable as people wearing blue.

By wearing certain colors, you invite certain things to happen. Some colors will attract, others will repel. Some colors will protect, others will cause danger. Even more important than wearing colors is the use of color magick with candles.

Thirteen Magickal Colors

White   Purity of heart, the Higher Self, cleanliness, spirituality, sacredness, the path of truth, a virgin.

Yellow   Healing, health matters, intelligence, learning, the ability to sell yourself in high regards, happiness.

Blue   Protection, calming energy, peace of mind, tranquility, reassurance, creativity.

Green Money of all kinds, prosperity, employment, success in business, growth, fertility, attainment of goals.

Pink True love, romance, healing of the emotions, beauty, caring, nurturing, maturity, and unconditional love.

Red Energy, strength, passion, fast action, anger, lust, industriousness, danger, impulsiveness.

Orange Attraction, compulsion, attainment of business goals, property dealings, and legal matters.

Purple Power, control of psychic energy, intuition, influence over other people, self-assurance, and royalty.

Gold Fortune, complete success in any endeavor, higher than middle-class living, accomplishment, and reverence.

Silver Psychometrics, dreams, astral projection, and money in investments and properties.

Brown Marriage, the union of two souls, the hearth and the home, stable friendships, bonded and united energies.

Gray To repel, to send away energies that disrupt harmony, to reject, to banish, to return negativity to its source.

Black The power of all combined colors, to protect in ways of secrecy, negativity, and binding energy.

How to Perform Color Magick

Obtain any colored paper and cut it into squares approximately three inches by three inches. The eight basic colors you will need are: white, yellow, blue, pink, red, orange, green, and purple. Write your wishes on the corresponding color, that is, blue paper for protection, green for money, and so forth. At the bottom of the paper, end each wish with "So Mote It Be." Fold the parchment corner-to-corner so that it forms a triangle. Anoint the three corners lightly with a corresponding magickal oil, that is, with white use Angel oil, with pink use Lover's oil, and so forth. Using the flame of the Unity candle, ignite the parchments one by one. Recite: *"I cast into this fire, the fulfillment of my desire. So Mote It Be.*" Drop the burning parchment into the cauldron. Do this for each color.

NOTE: At the end of every ritual that involves burning, the ashes should be disposed of in a natural way and also according to the element for that day. Example: If the day of the week is in Pisces, scatter the ashes into water because Pisces is a water sign. See chapter 5 for reading the magickal calendar.

Example of a wish writing:

(Using pink paper) *I ask for unconditional love to be in my life. I ask to feel beautiful in every way. I ask that only good, solid friendships be mine. So Mote It Be.*

Candles

Candle magick has been in existence since the creation of candles themselves. The color of the candle represents the intent of the spell. It is as important as the prayer/incantation that goes with it. The best magickal candles are made of 100 percent beeswax.

Male Image Candle   Female Image Candle

When purchasing magickal candles, it is important to look for solid-colored candles. These can be difficult to find. One example of a solid candle is the small votive, which sells for about fifty cents. Another solid candle is the tall taper, which ranges in size and price.

These candles are usually solid in color and excellent for one-time spells. A lot of candles are a certain color on the outside, but the inside of the candle is white. Because of packaging, a person often cannot see whether the candle is solid in color. I highly recommend purchasing magickal candles at an occult supply store. Not only is the color solid, but the candle is made on the correct moon phase to correspond with the magickal intent.

A Witch can also make her own magick candles. I have made my own and I have also purchased magickal candles at an occult store. Both candles are equal in power and effect. Some Witches will include special herbs and stones to increase the power when they make their own candles. A word of caution, however: *Since many herbs are highly flammable, your candle may explode.* Never leave candles burning unattended.

There is a large variety of magickal candles, and all are unique in their own right. There are seven-knob wishing candles, glass-contained candles, image candles, globe candles, and so forth. The image candle is one of my favorites. It is a candle shaped in the form of a male or female body. The purpose of this type of candle can vary from love magick to prosperity. These candles are highly effective.

To anoint your candle, select a proper magickal oil corresponding to your magickal intent. Either place the oil in the well of the candle (the center around the wick) or rub the oil around the outside of the candle. Please realize that *magickal oil is also highly flammable.* A few drops of oil will go a long way. The proper oil, along with the proper-colored candle, will definitely open the Universe for what you are asking. Almost every single spell will evolve around the magickal candle. Once a candle has been anointed and used for one specific purpose, it cannot be reused to make something else happen. Once the spell has been cast, the candle belongs to that specific spell. Use different candles for different spells.

The parchment (paper) used in magick is also color-coordinated. When casting for a specific purpose, make sure the color of the paper matches the candle.

The Mamas and the Papas

Image magick is a strong tool in spell casting. Image magick consists of making an object to resemble a person. Outsiders to the craft refer to these as "Voodoo dolls." The correct terms are *Mommets* and *Poppets.* Mommets are female and Poppets are male. Over the years, I have condensed the term to just *Poppets,* giving it no gender until the end of its creation. Poppets are usually made of cloth. If you are able to obtain an article of clothing from the individual, such as a sock or shirt, create your poppet from this. Some poppets are created from natural things, like cornhusks, potatoes, carrots, and so forth. (I think this is where Mr. Potato Head got his start.) Poppets can be created in different colors, depending on the intention. A green poppet will generate money, a pink poppet will generate love, and so on. The poppets purchased in occult stores are roughly generic, but they are purchased according to magickal intention. Homemade poppets should have as much detail as you can get. The clothing, perfumes, hair, and so forth, of the person should all be included. Leave an opening in the back of the poppet to stuff any remaining items. There should be eyes, mouth, and heart areas marked on it. Make the poppet as detailed as possible. All people poppets should have one head, two arms, and two legs. If you need to place specific genitals on the poppet, feel free to do so. Cotton batting will fill out the poppet to make it full and complete. Don't forget to sew up the back when you are finished stuffing it. Remember, *never* allow anyone who is outside of the craft to view a poppet. If a person knows you have a poppet of him or her, this will destroy its magick. Keep your poppets safely stored away or buried when they are no longer needed.

The Power of Magickal Stones

The most magickal elements and tools aiding a Witch are the common and natural resources the earth provides for us. Stones and gems are among these.

Remember to cleanse, consecrate, and empower these stones before using them. To cleanse, use a water and salt ritual. To consecrate, dedicate the stone to the magickal purpose and anoint it with the proper oil. To empower the stone, let it stand in the light of the full moon, then remove it before sunrise. The stone will absorb the power of the moon.

The size of the stone or gem is not important; what matters is the stone's vibration. Does it have positive energy for what you need it to do?

A wise Witch can make powerful magick with a stone if she knows how to use it. Some stones create energies for employment, while other stones vibrate to love. In order for the stone to work its magick, it must be with the person—either in a pocket, in a bag, or worn by the person. It does no good to have it sitting on your altar if you are at work. If you use the stones correctly, nothing will be impossible.

The following is a very brief list of magickal stones and gems and their uses.

Amber   Allows the body to heal itself by changing negative to positive energies. Increases physical vitality. Promotes unconditional love. Gives the ability to make correct choices. Has purifying and rebirthing energy.

Amethyst   Spirituality and contentment. A meditation stone. Protects against psychic attack. Aligns energies. Business will prosper. Stops addictions. Controls attitudes. Promotes calmness.

Apache Tears   Aids in times of grief and despair. Provides insight and acceptance. Promotes forgiveness. Increases analytical abilities and a true understanding of all things.

Apatite   Stimulates intelligence. Has healing properties. Stores information. Balances the emotions. Enhances creativity. Suppresses hunger. Aids deep meditation. Eliminates blockages. Fosters truth.

Aquamarine   Stone of courage. Stimulates rapid intelligence. Shields and protects. Enhances spiritual awareness and the

ability to process. Aids in past-life regression. Makes one gentle
and compassionate. Guards against injury.

Aventurine   Blocks others from reading your energy. Promotes
good decision-making skills and leadership qualities. Motivates
and pioneers new energies. Promotes employment. Propels
instincts.

Banded Amethyst   Strength and love. Provides positive answers.
Enhances knowledge of the arts. Is spiritually healing. Repels
negativity. Heals headaches and heals the lungs.

Black Obsidian   Produces sincerity. Removes disorders. Used in
gazing for a scrying tool and for divining. Increases creativity.
Promotes change to eliminate flaws. A grounding stone.
Provides protection.

Black Tourmaline   Energy deflector. Lifts the spirits. Balances the
chakras. Repels spells of magick, spirits, and entities. Increases
physical vitality. Provides protection. Awakens creativity.

Bloodstone   Stone of courage. Is grounding and centering.
Promotes realignment, harmony, adaptability, and unselfishness.
Clarifies spiritual truths. Gives direction. Stimulates mysticism.
Dispels bewilderment.

Calcite   Aids in memory areas. Generates electrical impulses that
release positive energies. Good for astral travel. Activates the
chakras. Heals kidneys, pancreas, and spleen.

Carnelian   Analytical. Precise. Awakens talents. Repels envy, fear,
rage, and sorrow. Stabilizes the home. Increases and attracts love.

Citrine   Totally free of any negativity. The merchant's stone.
Wealth and income are stimulated. Clarifies problems. Elevates
energy. Enhances endurance. Opens the solar plexus.

Clear Quartz   Amplifies energy. Creativity and mind power
become strong. Uses energy to help you learn and teach better.
All mind talents are magnified.

Coral   Quiets the emotions and brings inner peace. Compels
people and animals toward the possessor. Stimulates mysticism
and communication. Accelerates knowledge.

Crocoite   Aids in relaxation. Stimulates intuition. Helps recovery
from physical, mental, and emotional disorders. Aids in
creativity and sexual encounters.

Crystal Fluorite   Stone of discernment and attitude. Stops chaotic
energy. Stabilizes relationships. Promotes physical perfection and
flawless health.

Emerald   Stone of successful love. Makes one sensitive and loyal.
Ability to make correct and positive choices. Law and order of
the Universe. Helps in legal disputes. Eliminates negativity.

Garnet   The health and commitment stone. Enhances creative
and personal power. Promotes love, warmth, and
understanding. Has calming effects. Aids self-discovery. Balances
energy flow.

Green Fluorite   Diminishes trauma. Eliminates negativity. Heals
stomach disorders. Has cleansing and rational energies. Soothes
upsets and all other energies.

Green Tourmaline   Enables one to see with the heart. Aids healing
plants. Transforms negative energy to positive. Attracts
prosperity and abundance. Has healing energy for the eyes.

Hematite   The mind stone. Encouragement. A booster of
mathematical ability and dexterity. Promotes tranquillity and
knowledge. Repels nervousness and negativity.

Herkimer Diamond   Increases awareness. Clears unconscious
fears. The attunement stone. Emits a healing and loving energy.
Activates to the surrounding environment.

Jasper   Used for astral travel. A supreme nurturer. Conducts love
energy. Is protective. Keeps energy at high levels. Soothes the
nerves.

Jet   Pursuit of business and finances. Has a calming effect.
Dispels fear, violence, and illness. Releases migraines and
swellings.

King Cobra Jasper   A supreme nurturer. Celebrates isolation. Is
protective and helpful in hospitalization. Aids in mental
disorders.

Kunzite   Removes obstacles. A high meditative tool. Promotes
maturity. Shields unwanted energy. Enhances security. Makes
one sensitive and sensual. Deflects radiation. Stimulates the
mind. Keep it away from oracles.

Kyanite   Never needs clearing. Immediately aligns chakras.
Increases tranquility and calming energy. Dispels confusion. Has
a balancing and prophetic energy. Aids in dreams and in
grounding.

Labradorite   Protects the wearer from energy-stealers and energy
leaks. Has a sustaining and maintaining energy. Enhances
intuition, intelligence, precision, and uniqueness. Reduces stress
and anxiety.

Lapis Lazuli   Helps you to understand the mysteries of the
universe. Increases awareness and mysticism, emotional purity,
and mental clarity. Assists the third eye. Balances yin and yang.
Releases restraints.

Malachite   Stone of transformation. Clarifies emotions and
releases blocked memories. Enhances psychic powers. Increases
finances, wisdom, and strength.

Moonstone   Good for balancing. Make wishes with this stone
for what is actually needed. Promotes growth and change.
Provides protection during travel. Offers calmness and
awareness.

Moss Agate   Helps one to be agreeable and persuasive. Improves
the ego and a person's positive personality traits. Gives the
power of speed. Helps to control the weather and crops.

Paua   Aids in developing creative talents. Assists in
understanding a person's destiny. Adds clarity and insight.
Stimulates circulation.

Peacock Rock   Aids chakra alignment. Protects against negativity.
Heals the cells. Eliminates fever and swelling. Promotes
happiness. Unites the emotions with the mind.

Peridot   Energy is warm and friendly. Recognizes impairments.
Regulates all cycles. Provides protection and balancing. Heals
bruised egos. Aids recovery. Heals ulcers and stomach problems.

Purple Fluorite   Enhances intuition and strong psychic ability. Enhances the ability to organize and prioritize. Promotes healing of the bones. Helps to open the third eye.

Pyrite   Provides protection at all levels. Repels dangers. Aids perfection. Promotes love and friendship. Improves memory. Heals the lungs. Reduces fevers.

Red Jasper   Rectifies unjust circumstances. Provides rescue. Enhances the ability to remember dreams. Prevents setbacks. Promotes taking responsibility for one's own actions and consequences.

Rhodochrosite   Stone of love and balance. Generates pulsating electrical energy. Promotes healing through love energies. Attunes to the higher self. Removes denial. Eliminates problems.

Rhodonite   Stone of unconditional love. Fosters generosity of spirit. Removes blockages. Encourages brotherhood. Dispels anxiety. Has yin and yang energy. Aids in healing emphysema.

Rose Quartz   Stone of gentle love and spiritual attunement. Promotes art, music, and infinite beauty. Heals emotional wounds. Balances love. Increases calmness and clarity.

Ruby in Matrix   Star of fire and purity. Enhances refinement in love. Transmigration of love. Facilitates teaching and the high levels of psychic energy, as well as astral travel. The record keeper.

Smoky Quartz   Attunes to hand and feet chakras. Penetrates and dissolves anger and negativity. Relieves barriers. Eliminates willfulness. Activates intuition. Promotes pride.

Snowflake Obsidian   Aids in grounding in meditation. Opens the energy fields. Heals skin disorders. Makes communication easier. Stone of purity, love, and beauty.

Sodalite   Eliminates confusion. Helps one to attain purity of heart. Reveals truth. Stirs the emotions. One's goal and purpose are identified. Supports the sacred laws of the Universe.

Sunstone   Clears and energizes the chakras. Dissipates fears and relieves stress. Encourages independence. Provides luck in games of chance.

Tanzanite   High spiritual visions. Protection and safety. High
magick rituals. Discovers mysteries. Heals skin disorders.
Improves eyesight.

Tiger Eye   Promotes clarity in organizing, psychic abilities, and
discipline in sexual behavior and emotions. Increases awareness
of personal needs. Soothes turmoil.

Turquoise   Healing and cleansing. The stone actually changes
color when danger is near. Is grounding and protective. Helps
the intuition and creativity. Fosters peace, love, and harmony.
Aids in wisdom and trust.

MOON MAGICK

The magickal moon in its wax or wane,
Empowers the Witch to release or gain.
Moonbeams driving down the powers,
Reaching the Witch calling the Towers.
The waxing moon will restore or advance,
From crescent to circle it will enhance.
The waning moon will release and banish,
From full to absent it will vanish.
Embrace the nights and crown the days,
Chart the calendar and the olde ways.
The Crones will chatter and sing the tune,
For all the Witches to draw down the moon.

BELLADONNA

Moon Phases

The Moon is governed by the Goddess. It is the eternal symbol of life, death, and rebirth. The Moon is the magickal source of power to Witches. Even though the powers of the Moon are somewhat of an enigma, the Moon is predictable.

The Moon works on a cycle of approximately twenty-eight days, just like the menstrual cycle of women. Absorbing the Moon's energy is an age-old practice; women and men absorb the energy and it enables them to heal and nurture the sick.

The Moon exerts a powerful influence on people. For instance, not so long ago, people were believed to be moonstruck if they spent too much time beneath the luminous rays of the Moon. The word *lunatic* derives from the Latin word *luna*, meaning moon. The word means to have an ecstatic revelation or to become crazy. This proves that there is a very fine line between genius and madness. There was also a time when people believed in lycanthropy. Lycanthropy is the process of becoming a werewolf due to being bitten or scratched by a wolf. The transformation would occur on the night of the full Moon. The victim would sprout hair and fangs, and become obsessed with the taste of blood. A werewolf would have no control over his actions. The lunacy would override all consciousness. Whether or not one believes in werewolves or in being moonstruck, on one thing there is general agreement about the Moon: people are strangely affected by it.

The Moon controls our subconscious, our emotions, our psychic abilities, our motivation, and our thought processes. The Moon also controls and regulates the tides of the ocean. The expression *to draw down the Moon* means to tap and funnel the power and energies from the Moon, and to channel it to a specific magickal purpose.

To empower talismans, amulets, magickal stones, or any other magickal device, simply place the item in the light of the full Moon to absorb the rays. Remove the item before sunrise and place it in a dark area. This is to incubate the energies so the item will become powerful. A full ritual to charge a magickal device consists of three parts: First, cleanse the item with a salt and water ritual; second, consecrate the item, which means dedicate it to a specific intent; third, empower it with the Moon's energy.

Gives Good Fortune   Mars Seal of Protections   Seal of Hidden
in any Lottery   (Amulet)   Treasures
(Talisman)   (Talisman)

An amulet is a magickal charm that will protect or ward off evil or injury. An amulet will only work magick for the person who carries it, not necessarily for the person who charged it. A talisman works in the same manner as an amulet, but it is a magickal charm that will bring luck or power to the person who carries it. The primary difference between the amulet and talisman is the amulet will *repel* and the talisman will *compel*. Both amulets and talismans are made of some sort of metal or natural element, and they are inscribed with magickal symbols that only a Witch can properly decipher. Most of the symbols are of ancient seals, pictures, or codes. They are made at the right time of the Moon with the proper elements, but they are not charged until the Witch cleanses, consecrates, and empowers them.

When the Moon is eclipsing or when anything is obscuring the Moon's face, do not perform any magick whatsoever. The attempted magick would not work, and, in addition, it would be accompanied by a nasty sting of negativity that would not soon be forgotten. All magick should wait until after the eclipse is over. If clouds obscure the Moon and do not have any movement away from the Moon, do not perform any magick. If clouds are moving in and out from the face of the Moon, it is fine. The magick will still work and be positive.

The Moon has four quarters during a twenty-eight-day cycle. Even though there are four quarters, the Moon has only two phases. The two phases are the waxing and the waning. The waxing side of the Moon is the positive side. This is a time to invoke the *increase* of things. The waning side of the Moon is the negative side. This is a time to invoke the *decrease* of things, or simply wait and do nothing. The waxing Moon begins on the New Moon and ends approximately on the third day of the Full Moon. The waning Moon begins on approximately the third day of the Full Moon and ends on the New Moon. Both the waxing and waning have two quarters each.

The New Moon is also called the Dark of the Moon, or the Hare Moon. It is called the Hare Moon because in ancient times the rabbit was frequently hunted by the light of the Moon. When the Moon was dark (during the Hare Moon), rabbits could feast upon the land in relative safety because hunters could not see them.

The Full Moon and the Hare Moon last for almost three days. The second day of each is the most powerful time of the month. The Full Moon is the most powerful and the Hare Moon is the second most powerful. These days are the very highest points of magick in a twenty-eight-day cycle.

WAXING   FULL   WANING

The Waxing Moon   Growth, achievement, fortune, healing, gains,
increase.
The Waning Moon   Banishing, reducing, eliminating, minimizing,
decrease.

The powers of the Full Moon are unlimited. They can bring the most wonderful surge of luck and fortune, or they can be a nightmare. The effects are unpredictable. The wise Witch knows that the Moon is an ultimate source of power; it is to her advantage to harness it for positive use. People who work in hospital emergency rooms simply dread the days and nights of the Full Moon. Unusually high numbers of catastrophes occur during these days. People who are mentally deficient are also greatly affected on these days. What some people consider a monthly curse, the wise Witch considers to be a time of transfusion of power and energy.

Numerous factors are important in spell casting. The day of the week is important. The time is important. The astrological ruling sign is important. The most significant issue in spell casting, however, is the Moon phase. When the Moon is waxing, cast spells that bring increase. When the Moon is waning, cast spells that involve decrease. Magick during the waning Moon has been a very controversial point: Some Witches believe it is a time to rest and to perform no magick at all. I believe every single day is magickal. The time of rest is when there is no desire for increase or decrease. If situations are going well, then let them be.

Planets

All planets in our solar system have an effect on us. Each planet has a specific power and purpose. Each planet rules specific signs of the Zodiac as well. Astrology plays a significant role in magick. A Witch does not need to be an astrologer to master the knowledge; rather, a chart of tables will supply most of the information.

There are 365 days in a year. Each day is governed by a specific planet. Each day will also have a rotating Zodiac sign. The planets are consistent to their assigned days, but the Zodiac sign is constantly revolving. The Zodiac sign will stay in its ruling position for approximately two and one-half days. By knowing what sign is ruling for a specific day and also knowing what phase the Moon is in, the wise Witch knows what kind of spells are most positive for that day.

Even the hours of the day and night are ruled by specific planets. When selecting spells, it is important to cast them according to the best magickal hour, the best magickal day, and the best Zodiac sign. All of this information should be charted and placed in the Grimoire. These tables are very important when casting spells.

Each day of the week will also have a primary color. This can be coordinated with the spells, but it is only an option. The color magick should always coordinate to the intent of the spell, regardless of what the day's color is.

It is my opinion that astrology can benefit the wise Witch. By understanding the planets and the houses, we can easily see why we are the way we are and what events are likely to occur. We can also identify problem areas and figure out which tolls will help us.

The Thirteen Full Moons

January	The Wolf Moon
February	The Storm Moon
March	The Chaste Moon
April	The Seed Moon
May	The Lover's Moon
June	The Honey Moon
July	The Festive Moon
August	The Poet's Moon
September	The Fire Moon
October	The Harvest Moon
November	The Hunter's Moon
December	The Laughing Moon
The Thirteenth Moon	The Blue Moon

THE LUNAR CYCLE

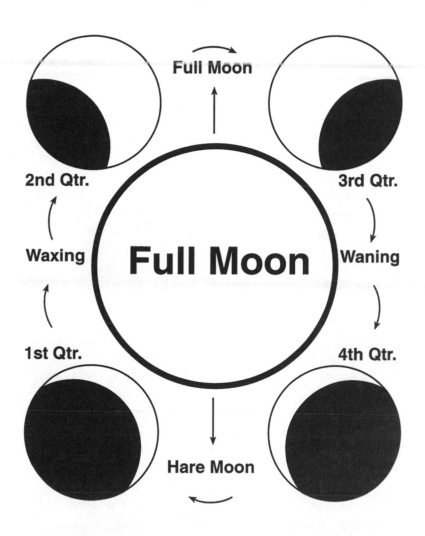

There are twelve to thirteen Full Moons every year. The month that has two Full Moons will have the Blue Moon. The Blue Moon is the second Full Moon of the same month.

Alternate Moon Names

January   Quiet Moon, Snow Moon, Cold Moon, Guardian Moon
February   Ice Moon, Horning Moon, Hunger Moon, Quickening Moon
March   Nymph Moon, Crow Moon, Dwarf Moon
April   Growing Moon, Planter's Moon, Baby Moon
May   Hare Moon, Merry Moon, Bright Moon, Flower Moon
June   Dyad Moon, Rose Moon, Marriage Moon
July   Mead Moon, Maiden Moon, Wort Moon, Thunder Moon
August   Corn Moon, Bay Moon, Ripening Moon
September   Barley Moon, Wine Moon, Autumn Moon
October   Blood Moon, Shedding Moon, Hallow Moon
November   Winter Moon, Dead Moon, Frost Moon
December   Oak Moon, Yule Moon, Pepper Moon

The Moons can take on other names, but these are the most common names corresponding to each month. According to the magickal calendar, the name of the Moon may vary if the Full Moon falls on a specific day of the Zodiac or a specific element.
For example:

Seed Moon   Full Moon on a fruitful sign of the Zodiac.
Philosopher's Moon   Full Moon in Sagittarius.
Harvest Moon   First Full Moon after the autumn equinox.
Lover's Moon   Full Moon in Scorpio.
Snow Moon   First Full Moon in the first month of snow.
Hearth Moon   Full Moon in Cancer.
Yule Moon   If the Full Moon occurs during the week of Yule.
Sylph Moon   When the Full Moon is in an Air sign.
Nymph Moon   Full Moon during the Goddess's first trimester.

Maiden Moon   Full Moon during the Goddess's Mother Phase.
Hecate Moon   Full Moon during the Goddess's Croning Phase.

The Four Energy Currents

The Planting Time   Starts on the spring equinox. Peaks on the
first of May. Ends on June 19.
The Growing Time   Starts on the summer solstice. Peaks on the
first of August. Ends on September 20.
The Harvest Time   Starts on the autumn equinox. Peaks on the
first of November. Ends on December 20.
The Resting Time   Starts on the winter solstice. Peaks on the first
of February. Ends on March 20.

The Astrological Chart

To chart your own horoscope, you need the date of birth, the
time of birth, and the city and state in which you were born. It is
easier to feed this information into a computer and let it be charted
this way rather than charting it by hand. When your wheel is
printed, it will have twelve houses mapped out. Each house represents a certain aspect of life. Some houses will have planetary activity and others will be empty. If the house is empty, it is assumed
there will be minimal effect from those areas in your life.

THE PLANET SIGNS

MOON	☽	JUPITER	♃
SUN	☉	SATURN	♄
MERCURY	☿	URANUS	♅
VENUS	♀	NEPTUNE	♆
EARTH	⊕	PLUTO	♇
MARS	♂	NORTHERN NODE	☊

The Zodiac Table

Aries   Competitive, ruled by Mars, March 20–April 20, Fire.
Taurus   Practical, ruled by Venus, April 20–May 20, Earth.
Gemini   Dual, ruled by Mercury, May 21–June 20, Air.
Cancer   Traditional, ruled by Moon, June 21–July 22, Water.
Leo   Dramatic, ruled by Sun, July 23–August 22, Fire.
Virgo   Analytical, ruled by Mercury, August 23–September 22, Earth.
Libra   Sociable, ruled by Venus, September 23–October 22, Air.
Scorpio   Intense, ruled by Mars, October 23–November 22, Water.
Sagittarius   Energetic, ruled by Jupiter, November 23–December 21, Fire.
Capricorn   Cautious, ruled by Saturn, December 22–January 20, Earth.
Aquarius   Intelligent, ruled by Saturn, January 21–February 20, Air.
Pisces   Independent, ruled by Jupiter, February 21–March 20, Water.

The Angels That Guard the Zodiac

Aries	Machidiel	*Libra*	Uriel
Taurus	Asmodel	*Scorpio*	Barbiel
Gemini	Ambriel	*Sagittarius*	Adnachiel
Cancer	Muriel	*Capricorn*	Hanael
Leo	Verchiel	*Aquarius*	Gabriel
Virgo	Hamaliel	*Pisces*	Barchiel

The Planets

The Sun   Involves ego, identity, happiness, and healing.
The Moon   Involves emotions, erratic powers, memories, and the mind.

The Earth   Involves stability, grounding, blessings, and natural abilities.
Mercury   Involves communications, intelligence, skills, and social activities.
Venus   Involves love, pleasures, fine arts, and beauty.
Mars   Involves energy, challenges, competition, and sports.
Jupiter   Involves expansion, religion, happiness, and growth.
Saturn   Involves restrictions, responsibilities, reality, and the inability to grow.
Uranus   Involves originality, science, progress, and uniqueness.
Neptune   Involves escapism, dreams, illusions, and inspirations.
Pluto   Involves power, rebirth, resources, and potential.

The Zodiac Signs

ARIES	♈	LIBRA	♎
TAURUS	♉	SCORPIO	♏
GEMINI	♊	SAGITTARIUS	♐
CANCER	♋	CAPRICORN	♑
LEO	♌	AQUARIUS	♒
VIRGO	♍	PISCES	♓

Astrological Houses

First House   Identity, appearance, and personality
Second House   Possessions, money, and tools
Third House   Communications, vocal and musical talents
Fourth House   Family, security, and childhood
Fifth House   Talents, romance, and creativity
Sixth House   Employment, service, and health
Seventh House   Marriage, partnership, and union
Eighth House   Regeneration, soul, death, and sex
Ninth House   Education, travel, and philosophy

Tenth House Fame, achievement, and mastery
Eleventh House Friends, hopes, and wishes
Twelfth House Hell house. Sacrifice, solitude, and the unknown

Astrology can help the Witch determine what areas of life are the strongest and what areas are the weakest. The main chart consists of a wheel. The wheel tells which planets are in which house.

The Four Elements

Certain elements have power in specific areas of life. Because these elements have power, it is important to use them to the highest advantage in magick.

EARTH   Governs fertility, jobs, promotions, money, business, investments, material objects, agriculture, health foods, stock market, ecology, antiques, old age, and progress.

AIR   Governs school, memory, intelligence, teaching, tests, divining, communications, travel, writing, organizing, drug addiction, and music.

FIRE   Governs success, sex, banishing illness, military, conflicts, protection, courts, competition, dowsing, treasure hunting, gambling, athletics, strength, terrorism, and war.

WATER   Governs love, friendship, partnership, unions, affection, negotiations, beauty, rest, meditation, spirituality, healing wounds, restoring cell growth, children, childbirth, home, family, fishing, ancestors, medicine, hospitals, compassion, and clairvoyance.

Fire   Free will. Active. Aries, Leo, and Sagittarius.
Earth   Body. Reactive. Taurus, Virgo, and Capricorn.
Air   Mind. Active. Gemini, Libra, and Aquarius.
Water   Emotion. Reactive. Cancer, Scorpio, and Pisces.

The Quadrants

Other Names for Quadrants: Towers, Quarters, Corners, and Elementals

Element	Direction	Season	Angel
Earth	North	Spring	Uriel
Air	East	Summer	Raphael
Fire	South	Autumn	Michael
Water	West	Winter	Gabriel

Calendars

The Waxing and Waning Zodiac

On the Magickal Calendar, the Moon phase and the ruling Zodiac are placed on each day. This will tell what Magickal range is good. The word *barren* refers to the still or absent power. The word *fruitful* refers to the growing and expanding power.

Aries Waxing (Barren)   Found money. Intense activities. Collecting herbs to banish illness.

Aries Waning (Barren)   Banish unwanted habits such as drugs, alcohol, smoking, overeating, spending, gambling, and so forth.

Taurus Waxing (Fruitful)   Begin new relationships. Starting of new projects. The beginning of new goals.

Taurus Waning (Fruitful)   A time to increase patience. Long-term goals should be analyzed. Strategy.

Gemini Waxing (Barren)   Work on communications, writing, singing, and so forth. Making the choices between two or more things.

Gemini Waning (Barren)   Banishment of all negative energy and negative things. Banishment of the double-edged sword.

Cancer Waxing (Fruitful)   New issues and new ideas will now
flow smoothly. Conception of children. Flow and progress.
Cancer Waning (Fruitful)   Break through obstacles with new
ideas. New path for all blocked roads.
Leo Waxing (Barren)   Finding of lost objects. Finding truth in all
matters. Seeking what cannot be seen.
Leo Waning (Barren)   Protection for family. Protection for
possessions. Protection for all safety matters.
Virgo Waxing (Barren)   Fresh outlook on life. Use independence
and logic to help yourself and others.
Virgo Waning (Barren)   Banishing grief, anger, burdens, and
stagnation. Best time to release anything that is bad.
Libra Waxing (Fruitful)   Artistry and designing. A time for
creativity and adventures.
Libra Waning (Fruitful)   A time for seclusion. Contemplation.
Daydreams and wishful outlook.
Scorpio Waxing (Fruitful)   Start actions that will produce results.
Assertiveness.
Scorpio Waning (Fruitful)   Find new solutions to existing
problems. A time to correct past mistakes.
Sagittarius Waxing (Barren)   Use information of the past to solve
the future. Resort to wisdom.
Sagittarius Waning (Barren)   Banishment of negative forces in
and around the home. Banishment of self-destruction.
Capricorn Waxing (Fruitful)   Take one step at a time for assured
outcome. Make short-term goals that lead to long-term goals.
Capricorn Waning (Fruitful)   Solidify actions. Move and calculate
slowly. Read the fine print.
Aquarius Waxing (Barren)   Rid the debts. Consolidate. Regroup.
Abandon the negative forces.
Aquarius Waning (Barren)   Banish all unwanted ghosts and all
unwanted astral energy. Break the energy stealers.
Pisces Waxing (Fruitful)   New beginnings with many different
branches. Expansion of positive growth.
Pisces Waning (Fruitful)   Use accessories and Magick to aid all
endeavors. Individual practice. Summons all positive powers.

How the Zodiac Rules the Body

Aries	Head, face, and brain
Taurus	Neck, throat, ears, and cerebellum
Gemini	Arms, hands, shoulders, lungs, and blood
Cancer	Chest, stomach, and digestive organs
Leo	Heart, spine, and back
Virgo	Bowels, intestines, and abdomen
Libra	Kidneys and the skin
Scorpio	Genitals, bladder, and appendix
Sagittarius	Hips and thighs
Capricorn	Knees, bones, and jointed areas
Aquarius	Legs and ankles
Pisces	Feet and toes

Magickal Table of Days

SUNDAY   Ruled by the Sun. Assigned color is yellow.
   Magickal Potential   Dealings with employers, promotions, friendships, healings, divine power, labor, and world leaders.

MONDAY   Ruled by the Moon. Assigned color is orange. *Magickal Potential*   Dealings with the home, family, agriculture, cooking, clairvoyance, medicine, dreams, and the sea.

TUESDAY   Ruled by Mars. Assigned color is red.
   Magickal Potential   Dealings with conflict, surgery, lust, physical strength, courage, politics, debates, athletics, war, contests, and issues dealing with people's rights.

WEDNESDAY   Ruled by Mercury. Assigned color is green.
   Magickal Potential   Dealings with studies, learning, teaching, divining, predictions, self-improvement, the community, the mind, and celibacy.

THURSDAY   Ruled by Jupiter. Assigned color is blue.
   Magickal Potential   Dealings with wealth, poverty, moneys of any kind, legal matters, luck, materialism, and gains.

FRIDAY   Ruled by Venus. Assigned color is indigo.
   Magickal Potential   Dealings with love, pleasure, art, music, partnerships, women in general, and beauty.

SATURDAY   Ruled by Saturn. Assigned color is violet.
Magickal Potential   Dealings with buildings, elderly, funerals,
wills, reincarnation, destroying disease and pests, termination,
confinement, and death.

EXAMPLE OF THE MAGICKAL CALENDAR

SUN	MON	TUES	WED	THURS	FRI	SAT
		WAX 1 TAU	WAX 2 TAU	WAX 3 T/GEM	WAX 4 GEM	WAX 5 G/CAN
WAX 6 CAN	WAX 7 C/LEO	WAX 8 LEO	WAX 9 LEO	WAX 10 VIR	WAX 11 VIR	WAX 12 V/LIB
WAX 13 LIB	FULL 14 L/SCO	WANE 15 SCO	WANE 16 SCO	WANE 17 SAG	WANE 18 SAG	WANE 19 S/CAP
WANE 20 CAP	WANE 21 CAP	WANE 22 AQU	WANE 23 AQU	WANE 24 A/PIS	WANE 25 PIS	WANE 26 PIS
WANE 27 ARI	WANE 28 ARI	HARE 29 A/TAU	WAX 30 TAU	WAX 31 TAU		

Tuesday First WAX/TAU   Magickal for spells dealing with
contests.
Wednesday Second WAX/TAU   Magickal for spells to improve
psychic skill.

Thursday Third WAX/T/GEM   Magickal for spells to write
music.
Friday Fourth WAX/GEM   Magickal for spells dealing with love.
Saturday Fifth WAX/G/CAN   Magickal for spells dealing in
legalities.
Sunday Sixth WAX/CAN   Magickal for job promotions.
Monday Seventh WAX/C/LEO   Magickal for healing.
Tuesday Eighth WAX/LEO   Magickal for courage.

TABLE OF MAGICKAL HOURS OF THE DAY

Hours

AM	*Sun.*	*Mon.*	*Tues.*	*Wed.*	*Thurs.*	*Fri.*	*Sat.*
1:00	Sun	Moon	Mars	Merc.	Jup.	Ven.	Sat.
2:00	Ven.	Sat.	Sun	Moon	Mars	Merc.	Jup.
3:00	Merc.	Jup.	Ven.	Sat.	Sun	Moon	Mars
4:00	Moon	Mars	Merc.	Jup.	Ven.	Sat.	Sun
5:00	Sat.	Sun	Moon	Mars	Merc.	Jup.	Ven.
6:00	Jup.	Ven.	Sat.	Sun	Moon	Mars	Merc.
7:00	Mars	Merc.	Jup.	Ven.	Sat.	Sun	Moon
8:00	Sun	Moon	Mars	Merc.	Jup.	Ven.	Sat.
9:00	Ven.	Sat.	Sun	Moon	Mars	Merc.	Jup.
10:00	Merc.	Jup.	Ven.	Sat.	Sun	Moon	Mars
11:00	Moon	Mars	Merc.	Jup.	Ven.	Sat.	Sun
12:00	Sat.	Sun	Moon	Mars	Merc.	Jup.	Ven.

TABLE OF MAGICKAL HOURS OF THE NIGHT

Hours

PM	Sun.	Mon.	Tues.	Wed.	Thurs.	Fri.	Sat.
1:00	Jup.	Ven.	Sat.	Sun	Moon	Mars	Merc.
2:00	Mars	Merc.	Jup.	Ven.	Sat.	Sun	Moon
3:00	Sun	Moon	Mars	Merc.	Jup.	Ven.	Sat.
4:00	Ven.	Sat.	Sun	Moon	Mars	Merc.	Jup.
5:00	Merc.	Jup.	Ven.	Sat.	Sun	Moon	Mars
6:00	Moon	Mars	Merc.	Jup.	Ven.	Sat.	Sun
7:00	Sat.	Sun	Moon	Mars	Merc.	Jup.	Ven.
8:00	Jup.	Ven.	Sat.	Sun	Moon	Mars	Merc.
9:00	Mars	Merc.	Jup.	Ven.	Sat.	Sun	Moon
10:00	Sun	Moon	Mars	Merc.	Jup.	Ven.	Sat.
11:00	Ven.	Sat.	Sun	Moon	Mars	Merc.	Jup.
12:00	Merc.	Jup.	Ven.	Sat.	Sun	Moon	Mars

6

HERBS, ⊕ILS, AND INCENSES

Smoking ashes and fragrant blooms,
All blended together beneath the moon.
A pinch of this, a dash of that,
Stir with whisker from a cat.
Eye of Newt and Dead Man's fear,
Brew the root with Seven Job's Tears.
Cast them deosil by the fume,
Sprinkle on whisk of Witch's broom.

BELLADONNA

Alchemy

Every good Witch is somewhat of a chemist. She puts together herbs, oils, and incenses to bring about a magickal change. Witches are often referred to as alchemists. An alchemist is a person who can take something of a specific element and change it into something better, with undertones of magickal transformation.

Alchemy has been practiced as an oral tradition since 1000 B.C. in almost every culture of the world. Alchemists were reputed to know the ingredients for the Elixir of Life, also called the recipe for immortality. Alchemists had the reputation for changing base metals into gold or silver. As science expanded, the secrets of true alchemy have waned greatly. By the nineteenth century alchemy was for the most part discredited and reduced to a pseudoscience.

Alchemy is still alive today in the Wiccan tradition. Through the passage of time many valuable secrets have been lost, but some still remain. The Wiccan society practices and retains these secrets in a very protected way. It is our hope to pass these on to the Witches of the future. The most positive side of alchemy is knowing that safe and proper experimentation can lead to miracles.

Alchemy is experimentation and is not intended to replace science or modern medicine. Alchemy is an ancient practice and is not restricted to the medical areas. If a person is in need of medical attention, do not assume that alchemy is the answer. It is to be considered an alternative method, just like herbal remedies. Understanding the magickal properties is a real key. With proper herbs, timing, and the use of elements and rituals, many modern-day miracles can happen. Alchemy is not only a part of healing, but it is also capable of having an impact in every area of our lives.

Herbs, plants, and botanicals are essential in magick. Each one has a ruling planet and a ruling element. A lot of herbs, plants, and botanicals have more than just one ruling planet and element. It is important to know this because the combination of specific planets with specific elements can cause certain effects and vibrations. The growth of plants, herbs, and botanicals and their harvesting merit a lesson in themselves. I highly recommend purchasing these items from an organic market, a health food store, or an occult store. When purchasing herbs at the grocery store, the Witch has no idea how long the herb has been on the shelf and it may not have any life force left in it. The fresher the herb, plant, and botanical, the more power it has. The more power your spell has, the more likely its success.

From plants, herbs, and botanicals evolve gums, resins, oils, extracts, roots, beans, wood, flower, bark, and powders. All of these products are valuable.

A mortar and a pestle are used by alchemists and Witches alike. These necessary tools can create herbal blends or mash and grind herbs into fine powders. The mortar is an earthen bowl and the pestle is the heavy, blunt, rounded instrument used to mash. Almost every pharmacy will display a mortar and pestle as a sign of ancient medicine.

Many magickal things come from herbs, plants, and botanicals. These products are incenses, oils, inks, powders, tinctures, brews, potions, and ointments.

Mojo bags are small red flannel bags sewn with white thread. Mojos are most commonly known for carrying magickal mixtures of herbs. Native Americans carry a medicine bag with the same intention. The medicine bag is usually made of deerskin. Since Wiccans do not believe in harming any kind of animal, the red flannel bag is our tradition.

Incense

The most commonly used magickal incense is the powdered type. It can be used with or without a charcoal base. Powdered incenses are labeled by their magickal name, not necessarily by their magickal intent. To use powdered incense, scoop out about one teaspoon of incense and place it in a fireproof incense burner. Brass works very well. Shape the incense into a pyramid form, ignite the peak of the incense, and then blow out the flame.

Oils

The magickal oils correspond to the magickal incense. There are two kinds of magickal oils: essential oils and oil blends. Both are equally magickal, but the difference lies mainly in their strength. Essential oils are highly concentrated and some are absolute extracts. Essential oils are very strong and are *not recommended for use directly on the skin.* The oil blends, however, are suitable for the skin. The oil blends are combinations of essential oils mixed with a mineral or almond oil base. Both essential oils and oil blends have the same magickal properties and potential.

Inks

Magickal inks are used for magickal writings. They are called for in specific spells, along with the use of a feather quill and specific parchment-type paper. The ink that is created is usually permanent. I have made my own magickal inks and I have used regular ink pens, and I found both are equally magickal. When making magickal ink, it can be a lengthy and messy process. You can purchase magickal ink from an occult store.

Powders

Magickal powders are used in many ways. They are all talc-based and have specific herbs and oils added to make them magickal.

Some sachets are blended with powders. The magickal powders are very old methods of alchemy.

Tinctures

Magickal tinctures use alcohol or fresh spring water as a base. The tinctures are usually used in healing, but can also be used in other areas. Tinctures are always in liquid form and the usual dosage is seven drops under the tongue. There are many, many tincture formulas the Witch can create. The Bach Flower Remedies are the finest tinctures I have ever tried. The Bach Flower Remedies are easier to access than creating your own and are also about the same price.

Magickal brews are concoctions of either foods or liquids and they are used with herbs. There should be no brew made that is ever poisonous. All brews should be edible or imbibable. Brews are usually very well prepared and have a lot of time invested in them. Potions, on the other hand, are almost always in liquid form and contain more magick than good taste.

Ointments

Magickal ointments use either a lard-type substance or beeswax as a base. Ointments are usually made for healing purposes, but I have seen them used for other reasons. They are created for all sorts of magickal intentions.

Herbs, plants, and botanicals usually have more than one common name. It is important to use a cross reference when you cannot find the specific herb that you need.

To suffumigate means to empower something with magickal smoke. When you are burning your magickal incense, wave your item in circles (clockwise) over the smoke to let it absorb the vibrations. Your item will have all the magickal benefits from this process. Most Witches suffumigate their talismans, amulets, and mojos.

The following charts will help you to understand herbs, plants, and botanicals and how to use them magickally. The Oils and

Incenses Guide will help you shop for the right ingredients for your spells. The Cross-Reference will help you identify multiple names for some of the oils and incenses.

When shopping at occult stores, do not expect too much help from any employee. A good Witch always knows what she is after, and bringing lists and cross-references will help.

The Celtic Tree

Alder	March 18–April 14
Willow	April 15–May 12
Hawthorn	May 13–June 9
Oak	June 10–July 7
Holly	July 8–August 4
Hazel	August 5–September 1
Vine	September 2–September 29
Ivy	September 30–October 27
Reed	October 28–November 24
Elder	November 25–December 22
Birch	December 23–January 20
Rowan	January 21–February 17
Ash	February 18–March 17

Rule of Thumb for Magickal Intent

Intent	Planet	Element
Banishing	Saturn	Fire
Beauty	Venus	Water
Courage	Mars	Fire
Divining	Mercury	Air
Employment	Sun/Jupiter	Earth
Energy	Sun/Mars	Fire

Intent	Planet	Element
Exorcism	Sun	Fire
Fertility	Moon	Earth
Friendship	Venus	Water
Happiness	Venus/Moon	Water
Healing	Moon/Mars	Fire/Water
Home	Saturn/Earth	Water/Earth
Love	Venus	Water
Peace	Moon/Venus	Any Element
Power	Sun/Mars	Fire
Prosperity	Jupiter	Earth
Protection	Sun/Mars	Fire
Psychic Power	Moon	Water
Purification	Saturn	Fire/Water
Sleep	Moon	Water
Success	Sun	Fire
Wisdom	Mercury	Air

Essential Oils

Allspice	Ginger	Sandalwood
Anise Seed	Juniper Berry	Siberian Fir
Bayleaf	Lavender Flower	Spearmint
Bergamot	Lemon	Spruce
Bitter Almond	Lemon Grass	Sweet Birch
Cajeput	Lime	Sweet Orange
Caraway	Mace	Tangerine
Cedarwood	Marjoram	Tarragon
Cinnamon	Nutmeg	Thuja
Citronella	Patchouli	Thyme, White
Clove Bud	Pennyroyal	Verbena
Coriander	Peppermint	Vetivert
Dill Weed	Rose Geranium	Wintergreen
Eucalyptus	Rosemary	Ylang Ylang
	Sage	

Magickal Herbs

Herb	Planet/Element	Properties
Absinthe	*See Wormwood*	
Acacia	Sun/Air	Protection, Clairvoyance, Love, Money
Adam and Eve Root	Venus/Water	Love
Acorns	Sun/Fire	Fertility
Adder's Tongue	Moon/Water	Healing
Agar-Agar	Mercury/Air	Fertility
Agaric	Mercury/Air	Psychic Powers
Agrimony	Jupiter/Air	Protection
Agueweed	Mars/Earth	Protection
Alfalfa	Venus/Earth	Money
Alkanet	Venus/Water	Purification, Prosperity
All Heal	*See Valerian*	
Allspice	Mars/Fire	Prosperity
Almond	Mercury/Air	Healing, Prosperity
Aloes	Moon/Water	Love, Healing
Althea	Venus/Water	Protection, Psychic Powers
Alum	Earth/Fire	Healing
Alyssum	Mars/Fire	Protection
Amaranth	Saturn/Fire	Healing, Protection
Anemone	Mars/Fire	Healing
Angelica	Sun/Fire	Protection, Psychic Powers
Anise	Jupiter/Air	Protection, Purification
Apple	Venus/Water	Love, Healing
Appleseed	*See Apple*	

Herb	Planet/Element	Properties
Apricot	Venus/Water	Love
Arabic, Gum	Sun/Air	Purification
Arbutus	Mars/Fire	Protection
Archangel Root	*See Angelica*	
Arnica	*See Wolf's Bane*	
Arrowroot	*See Yarrow*	
Arthritis Root	Venus/Water	Healing
Asafoetida	Mars/Fire	Protection, Purification
Ash	Sun/Fire	Protection, Prosperity
Aspen	Mercury/Air	Protection
Aster	Venus/Water	Love
Avens	Jupiter/Fire	Purification, Love
Avocado	Venus/Water	Love, Beauty
Balm of Gilead	Venus/Water	Love, Protection, Healing
Bamboo	Mercury/Air	Protection, Luck
Banana	Venus/Water	Love, Prosperity
Banyan	Jupiter/Air	Luck
Barberry	Venus/Sun	Love, Healing, Prosperity
Barley	Venus/Earth	Love, Healing, Protection
Basil	Mars/Fire	Exorcism, Protection, Prosperity
Bayberry	Sun/Fire	Protection, Prosperity
Baylaurel	*See Bayleaf*	
Bayleaf	Sun/Fire	Protection, Purification, Healing

Herb	Planet/Element	Properties
Bean	Mercury/Air	Protection, Exorcism, Peace
Bedstraw	Venus/Water	Love
Beech	Saturn/Air	Wishing
Beet	Saturn/Earth	Love
Belladonna (*Poison*)	Saturn/Water	*Avoid using this*
Benzoin	Sun/Air	Purification, Prosperity, Healing
Bergamot, Orange	Mercury/Air	Prosperity
Be Still (*Poison*)	Use as a talisman for luck *only*	
Beth	*See Trillium*	
Betony, Wood	Jupiter/Fire	Protection, Purification, Love, Prosperity
Birch	Venus/Water	Protection, Purification, Exorcism
Bistort	Saturn/Earth	Psychic Power
Bitter Root	*See Gentian*	
Bittersweet	Mercury/Air	Protection, Healing
Blackberry	Venus/Water	Healing, Money, Protection
Black Cohosh	Mars/Fire	Love, Protection, Power
Black Snakeroot	*See Black Cohosh*	
Bladderwrack	Moon/Water	Protection, Prosperity, Psychic Power
Bleeding Heart	Venus/Water	Love

Herb	Planet/Element	Properties
Blessed Thistle	Mars/Fire	Healing, Mind Power, Protection, Luck
Bloodroot	Mars/Fire	Love, Compelling
Blow Balls	See Dandelions	
Bluebell	Mercury/Air	Luck
Blueberry	Saturn/Earth	Protection
Blue Cohosh	Venus/Water	Healing
Blue Flag (Poison)	Venus/Water	Prosperity
Bodhi	Jupiter/Air	Protection, Psychic Power
Boldo	Mars/Fire	Protection
Boneset	Saturn/Water	Protection, Exorcism
Borage	Jupiter/Air	Courage, Psychic Power
Bracken	Mercury/Air	Healing, Psychic Power
Brazil Nut	Mercury/Air	Love
Briony	Mars/Fire	Prosperity, Protection
Bromeliad	Sun/Air	Protection, Prosperity
Broomtops	Mercury/Air	Purification, Protection, Divining
Buchu	Moon/Water	Psychic Power
Buckeyes	See Horse Chestnut	
Buckthorn	Saturn/Water	Protection, Exorcism, Legal Aid

Herb	Planet/Element	Properties
Buckwheat	Venus/Water	Prosperity, Protection
Bugleweed	Moon/Water	Psychic Power
Burdock	Venus/Water	Protection, Healing
Cabbage	Moon/Water	Luck
Cactus	Mercury/Water	Protection
Calamus	Moon/Water	Protection, Healing, Prosperity
Calendula	*See Marigolds*	
Camellia	Moon/Water	Prosperity
Camphor	Moon/Water	Divining, Healing
Caper	Venus/Water	Love
Caraway	Mercury/Air	Protection, Healing
Cardamom	Venus/Water	Love
Carnation	Sun/Fire	Protection, Healing
Carob	Sun/Water	Healing, Protection
Carrot	Mars/Earth	Love
Cascara Sagrada	Jupiter/Fire	Legal Aid, Protection, Prosperity
Cashew	Sun/Fire	Prosperity
Cassia	*See Senna*	
Catnip	Venus/Water	Love, Happiness, Beauty, Cat Magick
Cattail	Mars/Fire	Love
Cayenne	Mars/Fire	Psychic Power, Compelling, Mind Power

Herb	Planet/Element	Properties
Cedar	Sun/Fire	Healing, Protection, Prosperity
Celandine	Sun/Fire	Protection, Legal Aid
Celery	Mercury/Fire	Love, Psychic Power
Centuary	Sun/Fire	Protection from Snakes
Chamomile	Sun/Water	Prosperity, Love, Sleep
Cherry	Venus/Water	Love, Divining, Healing
Chestnut	Jupiter/Fire	Love
Chickweed	Moon/Water	Love
Chickory	Sun/Air	Talisman for Luck, Compelling
Chili	Mars/Fire	Love
Chinaberry (*Poison*)	Mars/Fire	Mojo for Luck *only*
Chives	Moon/Water	Psychic Power, Prosperity
Chrysanthemum	Sun/Fire	Protection
Cinchona	Mars/Fire	Mojo for Luck, Protection
Cinnamon	Sun/Fire	Healing, Compelling, Psychic Power, Love
Cinquefoil	Jupiter/Fire	Prosperity, Protection, Sleep
Citron	Sun/Air	Psychic Power, Healing

Herb	Planet/Element	Properties
Cloth of Gold	Mercury/Air	Psychic Power
Clove	Jupiter/Fire	Protection, Exorcism, Love, Prosperity
Clover	Mercury/Air	Prosperity, Success, Protection, Luck
Club Moss	Moon/Water	Protection, Power, Psychic Power
Coconut	Moon/Water	Purification, Protection
Collinsonia	See Figwort	
Coltsfoot	Venus/Water	Love, Psychic Power
Columbine	Venus/Water	Love, Courage
Comfrey	Saturn/Water	Protection, Prosperity
Copal	Sun/Fire	Love, Purification
Coriander	Mars/Fire	Love, Healing
Corn	Venus/Earth	Protection, Luck, Divining, Love
Cornsilk	Venus/Earth	Healing
Cotton	Moon/Earth	Luck, Healing, Psychic Power, Divining
Couchgrass	See Witch grass	
Cowslip	Venus/Water	Healing, Divining
Cranesbill	See Geranium	
Crocus	Venus/Water	Love, Psychic Power
Cubeb	Mars/Fire	Love
Cuckoo Flower	Venus/Water	Love, Fertility

Herb	Planet/Element	Properties
Cucumber	Moon/Water	Healing, Fertility
Cumin	Mars/Fire	Protection, Exorcism, Love
Curry	Mars/Fire	Protection, Love
Cyclamen	Venus/Water	Fertility, Happiness, Love
Cypress	Saturn/Earth	Healing, Protection, Happiness
Daffodil	Venus/Water	Love, Luck, Fertility
Daisy	Venus/Water	Love, Fertility
Damiana	Mars/Fire	Love, Psychic Power
Dandelion	Jupiter/Air	Divining, Psychic Power, Wishes
Datura (*Poison*)	Venus/Water	Protection *used in Mojo only*
Deer's Tongue	Mars/Fire	Love, Psychic Power
Devil's Bit	Mars/Fire	Protection, Exorcism, Love
Devil's Claw	*See Yarrow*	
Devil's Shoestring	Mars/Fire	Protection, Luck, Prosperity
Dill	Mercury/Fire	Protection, Prosperity, Love
Dittany of Crete	Venus/Water	Psychic Power
Dock	Jupiter/Air	Healing, Prosperity, Fertility
Dodder	Saturn/Water	Love, Divining

Herb	Planet/Element	Properties
Dogbane	Venus/Water	Love
Dogwood	Saturn/Air	Protection
Dragon's Blood	Mars/Fire	Love, Protection, Exorcism
Dulse	Moon/Water	Love, Psychic Power
Dutchman's Breeches	Venus/Fire	Love, Compelling
Ebony	Mars/Fire	Protection, Power
Echinacea	Mars/Fire	Power
Elder	Venus/Water	Exorcism, Healing, Prosperity, Sleep
Elecampane	Mercury/Air	Love, Protection, Psychic Power
Elm	Saturn/Water	Love, Protection
Endive	Jupiter/Air	Love, Lust, Psychic Power
Ephedra	Sun/Fire	Weight Loss, Healing
Eryngo	Venus/Water	Luck, Love
Eucalyptus	Moon/Water	Healing, Protection
Eyebright	Sun/Air	Psychic Power, Healing
Fennel	Mercury/Fire	Protection, Healing, Purification
Fenugreek	Mercury/Air	Prosperity
Fern	Mercury/Air	Protection, Luck, Prosperity, Exorcism
Feverfew	Venus/Water	Protection, Healing

Herb	Planet/Element	Properties
Fig	Jupiter/Fire	Divining, Fertility, Love
Figwort	Venus/Water	Healing, Protection
Five Finger Grass	*See Cinquefoil*	
Flax	Mercury/Fire	Prosperity, Protection, Beauty, Healing
Fleabane	Venus/Water	Exorcism, Protection
Forget-Me-Not	Venus/Water	Love
Foxglove (*Poison*)	Venus/Water	Protection
Frankincense	Sun/Fire	Protection, Exorcism, Psychic Power
Fumitory	Saturn/Earth	Prosperity, Exorcism
Fuzzyweed	Mars/Fire	Love, Luck
Galangal	Mars/Fire	Protection, Love, Prosperity, Psychic Power
Gardenia	Moon/Water	Love, Healing
Garlic	Mars/Fire	Protection, Healing, Exorcism, Lust
Gentian	Mars/Fire	Love, Power
Geranium	Venus/Water	Fertility, Healing, Love, Protection
Ginger	Mars/Fire	Love, Prosperity, Success, Compelling
Ginseng	Sun/Fire	Love, Healing, Beauty, Protection, Lust

Herb	Planet/Element	Properties
Goat's Weed	See St. John's Wort	
Goat's Rue	Mercury/Air	Healing
Golden Bough	See Mistletoe	
Goldenrod	Venus/Air	Prosperity, Divining, Love
Goldenseal	Sun/Fire	Healing, Prosperity
Gorse	Mars/Fire	Protection, Prosperity
Gotu Kola	Mercury/Air	Psychic Power
Gourd	Moon/Water	Protection, Divining
Grains of Paradise	Mars/Fire	Love, Prosperity, Luck
Grape	Moon/Water	Fertility, Psychic Power, Healing, Prosperity
Grass	Saturn/Air	Psychic Power, Protection
Gravel Root	See Meadowsweet	
Ground Ivy	Jupiter/Water	Divining
Groundsel	Venus/Water	Healing
Guinea Grains	See Grains of Paradise	
Hawthorn	Mars/Fire	Fertility, Happiness
Hazel	Sun/Air	Luck, Fertility, Happiness
Heal-All	See Valerian	
Healing Hearts	See Pansy	
Heart's Ease	See Pansy	
Heather	Venus/Water	Protection, Luck, Psychic Power

Herb	Planet/Element	Properties
Heliotrope (*Poison*)	Sun/Fire	Exorcism, Psychic Power, Healing, Prosperity
Hellebore (*Poison*)	Saturn/Water	*Avoid*
Hemlock (*Poison*)	Saturn/Water	*Avoid*
Hemp	Saturn/Water	Healing, Psychic Power
Henbane (*Poison*)	Saturn/Water	*Avoid*
Henna	Mars/Fire	Healing
Hibiscus	Venus/Water	Love, Divining
Hickory	Mercury/Fire	Legal Aid
High John the Conqueror (*Poison*)	Mars/Fire	Prosperity, Love, Success, Power, Luck
Hollyhock	Mars/Fire	Protection, Psychic Power
Honesty	Moon/Earth	Prosperity, Protection
Honeysuckle	Jupiter/Earth	Prosperity, Psychic Power, Protection
Hops	Mars/Air	Healing, Sleep
Horehound	Mercury/Air	Protection, Exorcism, Healing, Psychic Power
Horse Chestnut (*Poison*)	Jupiter/Fire	Prosperity, Healing
Horse Radish	Mars/Fire	Purification, Exorcism, Protection

Herb	Planet/Element	Properties
Horsetail	Saturn/Earth	Fertility, Compelling
Houndstongue	Mars/Fire	Power
Houseleek	Jupiter/Air	Luck, Protection, Love
Huckleberry	Venus/Water	Luck, Protection, Love
Hyacinth	Venus/Water	Love, Protection, Happiness
Hydrangea	Jupiter/Water	Protection
Hyssop	Jupiter/Fire	Purification, Protection
Iceland Moss	Moon/Water	Healing
Indian Paint Brush	Venus/Water	Love, Divining
Iris	Venus/Water	Purification, Wisdom
Irish Moss	Moon/Water	Prosperity, Luck, Protection
Ivy	Saturn/Water	Protection, Healing
Jaborandi	Mars/Fire	Exorcism
Jalap/Jalop	*See High John the Conqueror*	
Jasmine	Moon/Water	Love, Prosperity, Psychic Power
Jezebel Root	Venus/Fire	Luck, Success, Compelling, Lust
Job's Tears	Mercury/Fire	Divining, Wishing, Luck
Joe-Pye Weed	Venus/Water	Love, Luck
Juniper Berry	Sun/Fire	Protection, Love, Exorcism, Healing

Herb	Planet/Element	Properties
Kava-Kava	Saturn/Water	Psychic Power, Protection, Luck
Kelp	*See Bladderwrack*	
Khus-Khus	*See Vetivert*	
Knot Grass	Saturn/Earth	Healing, Binding
Kola Nut	Mercury/Water	Healing
Ladykins	*See Mandrake*	
Lady's Mantle	Venus/Water	Love
Lady's Slipper	Saturn/Water	Protection
Lady's Thumb	Venus/Water	Love
Larch	Mars/Fire	Protection
Larkspur	Venus/Water	Healing, Protection
Lavender	Mercury/Air	Love, Power, Happiness, Protection
Leek	Mars/Fire	Love, Protection, Exorcism
Lemon	Sun/Water	Purity, Healing, Love
Lemon Balm	Sun/Water	Healing
Lemon Grass	Mercury/Air	Psychic, Protection
Lemon Peel	*See Lemon*	
Lemon Verbena	Mercury/Air	Purity, Love
Lettuce	Moon/Water	Protection, Love, Divining, Sleep
Licorice	Venus/Water	Love, Lust
Life-Everlasting	Moon/Water	Healing, Protection
Lilac	Venus/Water	Exorcism, Protection, Power

Herb	Planet/Element	Properties
Lily	Moon/Water	Protection, Peace, Psychic Power
Lily of the Valley	Mercury/Air	Psychic Power, Peace
Lime	Sun/Air	Healing, Love, Prosperity
Lime Peel	Sun/Air	Healing, Prosperity
Linden	Jupiter/Air	Protection, Love, Sleep, Luck
Liquidamber	Sun/Fire	Protection
Liverwort	Jupiter/Fire	Love
Lobelia (*Poison*)	Saturn/Water	Compelling
Loosestrife	Moon/Earth	Protection, Peace
Lotus Root	Moon/Water	Protection, Psychic Power
Lovage	Sun/Fire	Love
Love Seed	Venus/Water	Love
Low John	*See Galangal*	
Lucky Hand	Venus/Water	Prosperity, Employment, Luck
Lungwort	Moon/Water	Healing
Mace	Mercury/Air	Psychic Power
Magnolia	Venus/Earth	Protection, Love
Maguey	Mars/Fire	Lust
Mahogany	Mars/Fire	Protection
Maidenhair	Venus/Water	Love, Beauty
Male Fern	Mercury/Air	Love, Luck
Mallow	Moon/Water	Love, Protection, Exorcism, Psychic Power
Malt	*See Barley*	

Herb	Planet/Element	Properties
Mandrake (*Poison*)	Mercury/Fire	Power, Protection, Healing, Prosperity, Love
Maple	Jupiter/Air	Love, Prosperity,
Marigold	Sun/Fire	Protection, Prosperity, Psychic Power
Marjoram	Mercury/Air	Love, Prosperity, Protection, Healing
Masterwort	Mars/Fire	Protection, Prosperity
Master of the Woods	*See Woodruff*	
Mastic	Sun/Air	Psychic Power, Love, Lust
May Apple	*See Mandrake*	
Meadow Rue	Venus/Air	Love, Divining
Meadowsweet	Jupiter/Air	Love, Divining, Healing, Happiness
Mesquite	Moon/Water	Healing
Mimosa	Saturn/Water	Love, Psychic Power, Protection
Mint	Mercury/Air	Prosperity, Protection, Psychic Power, Healing, Exorcism
Mistletoe (*Poison*)	Sun/Air	Love, Fertility, Divining, Healing, Protection

Herb	Planet/Element	Properties
Moonwort	Moon/Water	Prosperity, Love
Morning Glory	Saturn/Water	Happiness, Peace
Moss	Saturn/Water	Luck, Prosperity
Motherwort	*See Meadowsweet*	
Mugwort	Venus/Earth	Strength, Psychic Power, Love, Healing, Protection
Mulberry	Mercury/Air	Protection, Power
Mullein	Saturn/Fire	Courage, Protection, Love, Exorcism, Divining
Mushroom	Moon/Water	Psychic Power
Mustard	Mars/Water	Fertility, Protection, Power, Psychic Power
Myrrh	Moon/Water	Protection, Exorcism, Healing
Myrtle	Venus/Water	Love, Fertility, Prosperity
Nettles	Mars/Fire	Exorcism, Healing, Protection, Beauty
Norfolk Island Pine	Mars/Fire	Protection
Nutmeg	Jupiter/Fire	Prosperity, Healing, Luck
Nuts	Venus/Water	Fertility, Prosperity, Love, Luck

Herb	Planet/Element	Properties
Oak	Sun/Fire	Protection, Healing, Divining, Prosperity, Luck
Oats	Venus/Earth	Prosperity
Oleander (Poison)	Saturn/Earth	Love sachets
Olive	Sun/Fire	Fertility, Healing, Protection, Power
Onion	Mars/Fire	Protection, Healing, Exorcism, Psychic Power, Prosperity, Love
Orange	Sun/Fire	Love, Divining, Compelling, Prosperity
Orchid	Venus/Water	Love
Oregon Grape	Earth/Water	Prosperity, Luck
Oregano	Mercury/Air	Prosperity, Love, Fertility
Orris Root	Venus/Water	Love, Protection, Divining
Palm	Sun/Air	Fertility
Pansy	Saturn/Water	Love, Divining
Papaya	Moon/Water	Love, Protection
Paprika	Mars/Fire	Compelling, Love
Papyrus	Mercury/Air	Protection
Parsley	Mercury/Air	Lust, Protection, Purification
Pascalite	Sun/Water	Protection, Peace
Passion Flower	Venus/Water	Love, Peace

Herb	Planet/Element	Properties
Patchouli	Saturn/Earth	Prosperity, Fertility, Love
Pea	Venus/Earth	Prosperity, Love
Peach	Venus/Water	Love, Exorcism, Fertility, Compelling
Pear	Venus/Water	Love, Lust
Pearl Moss	*See Irish Moss*	
Pecan	Mercury/Air	Prosperity, Employment
Pennyroyal	Mars/Fire	Power, Protection, Peace
Peony	Sun/Fire	Protection, Exorcism
Pepper, Black	Mars/Fire	Protection, Exorcism
Pepper, Red	Mars/Fire	Protection, Exorcism
Peppermint	Mercury/Fire	Purification, Love, Healing, Psychic Power
Peppertree	Sun/Fire	Prosperity, Passion
Pepperwort	Moon/Water	Purification
Periwinkle	Venus/Water	Love, Beauty
Persimmon	Venus/Water	Healing, Luck, Love
Pilewort	*See Celandine*	
Pilotweed	Saturn/Water	Protection
Pimento	Mars/Fire	Love
Pimpernel	Mercury/Air	Protection, Healing
Pine	Mars/Air	Healing, Fertility, Prosperity, Exorcism, Protection

Herb	Planet/Element	Properties
Pineapple	Sun/Fire	Luck, Prosperity, Love
Pink Root	Venus/Fire	Love
Pipsissewa	Sun/Water	Healing, Prosperity, Psychic Power
Plaintain	Venus/Earth	Healing, Power, Protection
Pleurisy Root	Mars/Fire	Healing Pleurisy
Plum	Venus/Water	Love, Protection
Plumeria	Venus/Water	Love
Poke	Mars/Fire	Strength, Protection
Pomegranate	Mercury/Fire	Prosperity, Divining
Poplar	Saturn/Water	Prosperity
Poppy	Moon/Water	Love, Prosperity, Sleep
Potato	Moon/Earth	Healing
Prickly Ash	Mars/Fire	Love
Primrose	Venus/Earth	Love, Protection
Princess Pine	Sun/Fire	Success
Purslane	Moon/Water	Love, Protection, Psychic Power
Quassia Chips	Venus/Water	Love
Queen of the Meadow	*See Meadowsweet*	
Quince	Saturn/Earth	Protection, Love, Happiness
Quinine	*See Cinchona*	
Radish	Mars/Fire	Protection
Ragweed	*See Ragwort*	
Ragwort	Venus/Water	Protection
Raspberry	Venus/Water	Protection, Love
Rattlesnake Root	Jupiter/Earth	Protection, Prosperity

Herb	Planet/Element	Properties
Red Clover	Sun/Fire	Healing, Beauty
Red Root	See Bloodroot	
Rhubarb	Venus/Earth	Protection
Rice	Sun/Air	Protection, Prosperity, Fertility
Rose	Venus/Water	Love, Divining, Psychic Power
Rose Hips	Venus/Water	Love
Rose of Jericho	Sun/Fire	Exorcism
Rosemary	Sun/Fire	Love, Protection, Healing
Rose of Sharon	Moon/Water	Healing, Fertility
Rowan	Sun/Fire	Psychic Power, Protection, Healing, Power
Rue	Mars/Fire	Healing, Exorcism, Love
Rye	Venus/Earth	Love
Safflower	Sun/Water	Healing
Saffron	Sun/Fire	Love, Healing, Psychic Power
Sage	Jupiter/Air	Wisdom, Protection, Wishes
Sagebrush	Venus/Earth	Purification, Exorcism
Saint John's Bread	See Basil	
Saint John's Wort	Moon/Water	Healing
Sanguinary	See Yarrow	
Sarsparilla	Jupiter/Fire	Love, Prosperity
Sassafras	Jupiter/Fire	Healing, Prosperity

Herb	Planet/Element	Properties
Savory	Mercury/Air	Mind Power
Saw Palmetto	Venus/Fire	Passion
Scullcap	Saturn/Water	Love
Senna	Mercury/Air	Love
Sesame	Sun/Fire	Prosperity, Love
Shallot	Mars/Fire	Purification
Shavegrass	*See Horsetail*	
Shepherd's Purse	Sun/Water	Healing, Beauty
Skunk Cabbage	Saturn/Water	Legal Aid
Slippery Elm	Saturn/Air	To Stop Gossip
Sloe	Mars/Fire	Exorcism, Protection
Smartweed	Jupiter/Earth	Prosperity
Snakehead Root	Mars/Fire	Legal Aid
Snake Root	Jupiter/Earth	Luck, Prosperity
Snake Root Black	Mars/Fire	Love, Prosperity
Snapdragon	Mars/Fire	Protection
Solomon's Seal	Saturn/Water	Protection, Exorcism
Sorrel	Venus/Earth	Healing
Southernwood	Mercury/Air	Love, Protection
Spearmint	Venus/Water	Love, Healing, Prosperity
Spiderwort	Venus/Water	Love
Spikenard	Venus/Water	Love, Healing
Squaw Root	*See Black Cohosh*	
Squill Root	Mars/Fire	Prosperity, Protection
Star Anise	Jupiter/Air	Psychic Power, Luck
Stillengia	Moon/Water	Psychic Power
Storax	*See Liquidamber*	
Straw	Sun/Earth	Luck

Herb	Planet/Element	Properties
Strawberry	Venus/Water	Love, Luck
Stone Root	Sun/Fire	Protection
Sugar Cane	Venus/Water	Love
Sumbul	Moon/Fire	Healing, Luck, Love, Psychic Power
Sunflower	Sun/Fire	Fertility, Healing, Wisdom
Sweet Flag	Sun/Fire	Success
Sweetgrass	Moon/Air	Compelling, Raising Spirits
Sweetpea	Venus/Water	Friendship, Courage
Tamarind	Saturn/Water	Love
Tamarisk	Saturn/Water	Protection, Exorcism
Tansy	Venus/Water	Healing
Tarragon	Mars/Fire	Psychic Power, Love, Protection
Tea	Sun/Fire	Prosperity
Thistle	Mars/Fire	Protection, Strength
Thyme	Venus/Water	Healing, Psychic Power, Love
Ti	Jupiter/Fire	Protection, Healing
Toadflax	Mars/Fire	Protection
Tobacco	Mars/Fire	Visions, Protection
Tomato	Venus/Water	Prosperity, Love
Tonka Bean	Venus/Water	Love, Prosperity, Wishes
Tormentil	Sun/Fire	Protection, Love
Trillium	Venus/Water	Prosperity, Love

Herb	Planet/Element	Properties
Tuberose	Venus/Water	Love, Peace
Tulip	Venus/Earth	Prosperity, Love, Protection
Turmeric	Sun/Water	Purification
Turnip	Moon/Earth	Protection
Unicorn	See Ague Root	
Uva Ursi (Poison)	Moon/Fire	Psychic Power
Valerian	Venus/Water	Love, Protection
Van Van	See Vervain	
Vanilla	Venus/Water	Love, Purification
Venus Fly Trap	Mars/Fire	Protection, Love
Verbena	Venus/Earth	Love, Money, Protection
Vervain	Venus/Earth	Love, Prosperity, Protection
Vetivert	Venus/Earth	Love, Prosperity
Violet	Venus/Water	Power, Love, Healing
Wahoo (Poison)	Mars/Fire	Protection, Success
Walnut	Sun/Fire	Healing, Wishes
Waxplant	Mercury/Air	Protection
Wheat	Venus/Earth	Fertility, Prosperity
Willow	Moon/Water	Love, Divining, Healing
Wintergreen	Moon/Water	Protection, Healing
Wish Bean	See Tonka Bean	
Wisteria	Mars/Fire	Psychic Power, Love, Protection
Witch Burrs	See Liquidamber	
Witch Grass	Jupiter/Water	Love, Happiness
Witch Hazel	Sun/Fire	Protection

Herb	Planet/Element	Properties
Wolf's Bane	Saturn/Water	Protection
Wonder of the World	*See Ginseng*	
Woodrose	Saturn/Water	Luck
Woodruff	Mars/Fire	Prosperity, Protection
Wormwood (*Poison*)	Mars/Fire	Psychic Power, Love, Protection
Yarrow	Venus/Water	Love, Psychic Power, Exorcism
Yellow Dock	*See Dock*	
Yellow Evening Primrose	Mars/Fire	Courage, Healing, Protection
Yerba Maté	Mars/Fire	Love, Lust
Yerba Santa	Venus/Water	Love, Beauty, Healing, Protection
Yew (*Poison*)	Saturn/Water	To Raise Spirits
Ylang Ylang	Venus/Water	Love, Happiness
Yohimbe (*Poison*)	Mars/Fire	Love, Lust
Yucca	Mars/Fire	Protection, Purification

Magickal Incenses, Oils, and Bath Salts

White

The following magickal ingredients can be found in most occult stores. Please check the cross-reference at the end for names used by alternative manufacturers.

Amulet (white/gray)   To charge with power, to cleanse and repel.
Angel Blessing (white)   To invoke the aid of the Angels.
Aura Cleansing (white)   To align and cleanse the chakras.

Banishing (white/gray)   To clear away all negative energies.
Criss-Cross (white/gray)   To repel all negative forces.
Devil's Trap (white/black)   To dissipate and remove Demons.
Drive and Bind (white/gray)   To keep all negative forces at bay.
Drive Away Evil (white/gray)   To banish negativity from homes.
Exodus (white)   To use on all unwanted conditions.
Forgiveness (white)   When you've transgressed and need
    forgiveness.
Holy Smoke (white)   To call upon the Angels for help.
Jinx Remover (white)   To break any hex that is negative.
Lily of the Valley (white)   To receive answers from the Angels.
Mist (white)   To cleanse a magick circle or altar.
Moonlight (white)   To empower with only white energies.
Mystic Veil (white/blue)   To be invisible on the astral plane.
New Life (white/yellow)   To overcome guilt, failure, and regret.
Purity (white)   To forgive and to be forgiven. Purity of heart.
Uncrossing (white)   To remove any hex, curse, or spell.
White Solstice (white)   For all Sabbats.

Blue

Astral Projection (blue)   Protected travel during an out-of-body
    experience.
Azure (blue/white)   For cleansing and protection.
Beneficial Dream (blue/purple)   Psychic visions and dreams.
Blue Dragon (blue/green)   Heavy protection during prosperity.
Blue Gypsy (blue)   Promotes intrigue, curiosity, and protection.
Blue Moon (blue/purple)   Enhances psychic powers and
    awareness.
Dove's Flight (blue/yellow)   Peace and protection during travels.
Dream (blue/purple)   To make positive dreams occur and come
    true.
Hypnotic (blue)   For safety and protection during hypnosis.
Lavender Blue (blue/purple)   For calm, subtle power.
Lotus (blue)   For heavy protection in all areas.
Meditation (blue)   For meditation and prayer.

Peace (blue)   To keep the mind and all surroundings serene.
Protection (blue)   For heavy protection.
Protection from Thieves (blue/gray)   To keep thieves at bay.
Summer Rain (blue/white)   To cleanse and to protect.
Tranquillity (blue/white)   To purify and protect with calmness.
Vision (blue)   For prophetic dreams and visions.
Wicca (blue/green)   To aid Witches in all endeavors.
Witching Well (blue/green)   To ensure bounty and resources.

Yellow

Angel Wings (yellow)   To have the Angels aid in healing.
Concentration (yellow)   For better memory and study habits.
Crystal Bell (yellow)   Good health.
Dancing Faeries (yellow)   To solicit the help of the Faeries.
Easy Life (yellow)   For positive attitudes and happiness.
Eucalyptus (yellow)   For physical and emotional healing.
Good Health (yellow)   To promote better health.
Happiness (yellow)   To bring about happiness and harmony.
Healing (yellow)   To mend and heal the afflicted.
High Meadows (yellow/gold)   For the Angels to assist in healing.
Joy (yellow)   To promote happiness, laughter, and joy.
Lemon Drops (yellow/purple)   To empower the mind energies.
Mediterranean Magick (yellow)   For the imagination.
Memory (yellow/purple)   To improve the memory and the mind.
Positive Attitude (yellow)   To bring about positive thinking and a
   positive attitude.
Radiant Health (yellow)   To glow with good health.
Spirit Guide (yellow)   To call upon your individual Guide.
Springtime (yellow)   To promote laughter and new wishes.
Sunshine (yellow)   To heal and cleanse with good health.
Temple of Light (yellow)   Sacred healing and also various types of
   ritual work.

Pink

Algiers (pink/orange)   To draw love with magnetic force.
Beloved (pink)   To promote love in all areas.
Blessed Be (pink/white/blue)   To have love, purity, and peace.
Catkins (pink)   For playfulness in areas of love.
Cupid (pink)   To have that special someone fall in love with you.
Dove's Blood (pink/white)   For pure, romantic love.
Fantasy (pink)   To make romantic dreams come true.
Friendship (pink)   To bless new and old friendships.
Goddess (pink)   To call upon the Goddess.
Handfast (pink)   To ensure a perfect marriage.
Irresistible (pink/red)   To make one irresistible.
Kitten Love (pink)   For a playful, romantic adventure.
Love Breaker (pink/gray)   To stop love and to stop love spells.
Lovely (pink)   To become more beautiful.
Lovers (pink/red)   For romantic love to blossom to its fullest.
Merry Meet (pink)   To promote frolic and friendships.
Pink Musk (pink/red)   To have encounters with the opposite sex.
Sweetheart (pink)   To promote lasting relationships.
Sweetpea (pink)   To start new relationships and adventures.
Venus (pink/red)   The effects range from beauty to divine love.

Red

Adam and Eve (red/pink)   For sensual activity.
Aphrosidia (red)   To seduce in every way.
Aphrodite (red)   To seduce and to conquer.
Arabian Nights (red)   To seduce and to inspire passion.
Bat's Blood (red)   For passion and lust.
Black Cat (red/gold)   To have enormous energies.
Cleopatra (red/pink)   To dominate and to have sexual activity.
Dragon's Blood (red/white)   To have control with good intentions.

Eve (red/pink)   To induce someone to be smitten with you and to seduce.

Fire of Passion (red)   To stir passion in yourself and others.

Flaming Heart (red)   To rekindle passions.

French Love (red/orange)   To draw sexual activity toward you.

Jezebel (red)   To seduce someone shamelessly.

Mandrake (red/pink/purple)   To have all that you desire.

Musk Mountain (red)   To seduce men.

Passion (red)   To arouse sexual excitement.

Q (red)   For the daring. Strength is also enhanced.

Rendezvous (red)   To promote the highest levels of sensuality.

Sheba (red)   Used only by women to seduce males.

Temptation (red)   To seduce women.

Orange

Attraction (orange)   To compel and to attract.

Autumn Aspen (orange/green)   To draw money into a home.

Be Mine (orange/pink/purple)   To bring the object of your desire toward you.

Bewitching (orange)   To entrance with the undertones of mystery.

Cinnabar (orange/red)   To draw by way of seducing.

Come to Me (orange/purple)   To compel with force.

Compelling (orange)   To compel and to attract.

Cornucopia (orange)   To single out and draw toward you.

Draw Across (orange)   To bring forward.

Drawing (orange)   To draw toward you.

Enchantment (orange/pink)   To radiate with beauty and to compel.

Follow Me (orange/purple)   To force the object of your desire toward you.

French Quarter Creole (orange)   To attract and to enhance.

Honeysuckle (orange)   To attract with gentle force.

Magnet (orange/brown)   To compel toward the home.

Nefertiti (orange)   To compel.

Scorpion (orange/purple) To compel with force.
Talisman (orange) To charge with compelling energies.
Tiger (orange/brown) To compel with warmth.
VooDoo Night (orange/red) To become irresistible.

Green

Antique Jade (green/white) For Angels to inspire generosity.
Bayberry (green) To promote growth of money.
Better Business (green/gold) To increase business and success.
Coins in a Fountain (green) For wishing prosperity into reality.
Emerald (green) For intense money and success.
Fast Luck (green) For fast luck and money.
Fertility (green) To become more fertile.
Forest Nymph (green) Prosperity by way of employment.
Good Luck (green) To have good luck in all endeavors.
Helping Hand (green/white/purple) To have abundance.
Huntress (green) To have all that you intend to have.
Jade (green) For vast wealth.
Lady Luck (green) To bring fortune when gambling or investing.
Lucky Hand (green) To have abundance in all endeavors.
Mermaid's Song (green/blue) For enrichment.
Money Drawing (green/orange) To draw cash into wallets.
Prosperity (green) To become prosperous and wealthy.
Quick Money (green) To draw money fast.
Verbena (green) To have steady employment.
Woodlands (green) To have steady employment.

Purple

Angel (purple) To invoke the aid of the Angels.
Bending (purple) To have the power to bend someone's will.
Controlling (purple) To control every situation.
Crucible (purple) The power to reverse the odds.
Do as I Say (purple) For total control.
Double Action (purple) To have twice the power.

High John the Conqueror (purple)   To have victory in all areas.
Invocation (purple)   For invoking the aid of the Quadrants.
Magick (purple)   To increase all magickal endeavors.
Moon (purple/silver)   To increase all psychic powers.
Oracle (purple)   To aid during divining.
Pearl (purple/white)   To solicit the Archangels.
Pharaoh (purple)   To overcome the control others have over you.
Prudence (purple)   To overcome bad spending habits.
Psychic (purple)   To aid in clairvoyance and the sixth sense.
Seven Powers (purple/gold)   To meet your highest desires.
Special Favors (purple)   To achieve the impossible.
Violet (purple)   For power and control.
Witch (purple)   Aids in castings and all magickal spells.
Wolf Song (purple)   For courage when under pressure.

Gold

All Hallows (gold)   For high-intensity rituals.
Amber (gold)   To promote self-confidence.
Cleomay (gold)   For success and abundance.
Golden Emerald (gold/green)   To ensure wealth.
Isis (gold)   To promote personal success.
King Solomon (gold)   For the wealth of wisdom.
Midas (gold)   For success and abundance.
Mojo (gold)   To obtain any high endeavor.
Myrrh (gold)   The pinnacle of success.
Sweet Clover (gold/green)   To believe and to become successful.
Success (gold)   To have complete and total success.
Van Van (gold/white)   Success that is empowered by Angels.

Brown

Almond Bounty (brown/green)   To have abundance in the home.
Cedarwood (brown)   For the sanctity of the marriage vows.
Covenstead (brown/blue)   To protect the ritual area.
Exorcism (brown/white/gray)   To rid all areas of negativity.

Frankincense (brown/gold)   To honor the home.
Hearthside (brown/pink)   To keep love in the family.
House Blessing (brown/white/blue)   To bless and protect the home.
India Bouquet (brown/yellow/pink)   To heal marital woes.
Knock at My Door (brown/pink)   To invite friends into your life.
Marriage Mind (brown/pink)   To inspire and bless marriages.
Ravenwood (brown)   To keep the home and the family together.
Stay at Home (brown)   To keep loved ones in the home.

Gray

JuJu (gray/white/purple)   High intensity for repelling.
Rose Cross (gray/white/blue)   To repel all negativity.
Satan Be Gone (gray/white)   To remove demons.
Spell Breaker (gray)   To undo magickal spells.
Widdershins (gray)   To reverse energies.

Black

Black Musk (black/red)   To make a situation explosive.
Dragon's Fire (black/red/purple)   To intensify.
Leopard (black/brown)   To have a behind-the-scenes effect.
Midnight (black)   To have a secret, intense power.
Obsidian (black)   For a combined energy effect.

To Aid in Legal Areas

Ambergris (purple/gold/brown)   To intensify when you know that
   you are in the right.
Black Candle Tobacco (purple/black/gold)   To win in court and to
   overcome legal problems.
Just Judge (gold/black/purple/orange)   To persuade the judge to
   be fair-minded.
Sage (gray/blue/black)   To protect from the wrath of an angry
   judge.
Snake (black/gold)   To aid in overcoming difficult court cases.

Cross Reference for Incense, Oils, and Bath Salts

AC/DC   Use Vision.
African Ju Ju   Use Ju Ju.
All Purpose   Use Temple of Light.
Altar   Use Temple of Light.
Animal   Use Tiger.
Anointing   Use Temple of Light.
As You Please   Use Compelling.
Autumn Leaves   Use Peace.
Bend Over   Use Bending.
Bible   Use King Solomon.
Big Money   Use Money Drawing.
Bingo   Use Good Luck.
Blessed Mary or *Blessed Virgin*   Use Blessed Be.
Buddha   Use Meditation.
Business   Use Better Business.
Candle   Use Temple of Light.
Can't Stay Away   Use Arabian Nights.
Chango Macho   Use Midas.
Chinese   Use Temple of Light.
Cleo May   Use Lovers.
Comfort   Use Easy Life.
Congo   Use Lavender Blue.
Conquering Glory   Use High John the Conqueror.
Court   Use Van Van.
Crab Apple   Use Peace.
Crown of Success   Use Success.
Dare to Win   Use Success.
Desire Me   Use Lovers.
Devil's Shoestring   Use High John the Conqueror combined with
   Talisman.
Devil's Master   Use Bending.
Divine Savior   Use Blessed Be.
Dream   Use Beneficial Dream.

Dressing   Use Temple of Light.
Enemy   Use Protection.
Evil Eye   Combine Protection with Dragon's Blood.
Fast Money   Use Quick Money.
Fiery Wall of Protection   Combine Dragon's Blood with
   Protection.
Financial Luck   Combine Talisman, Good Luck, and Money
   Drawing.
Fire of Love   Use Fire of Passion.
Flame of Desire   Use Passion.
Flaming Power   Use Power.
Forget Him/Her   Use New Life.
Four Leaf Clover   Use Good Luck.
Free from Evil   Use Devil's Trap.
French Love   Combine French Quarter Creole with Lovers.
Fruit of Life   Use Easy Life.
Gamblers   Use Lucky Hand.
Glory   Use Temple of Light.
Glow of Attraction   Use Attraction.
Go Away   Use Drive and Bind.
Gold and Silver   Use Midas.
Gris Gris   Use Talisman.
Guardian Angel   Use Angel.
Has No Hanna   Use Happiness.
Health   Use Healing.
Hebrew   Use King Solomon.
Hearts of Desire   Use Cupid.
Henry's Grass   Use Dragon's Blood.
Hex Breaking   Use Uncrossing.
High Altar   Use Temple of Light.
Hold My Man   Use India Bouquet.
Holy   Use Temple of Light.
Horn of Plenty   Use Prosperity with Cornucopia.
Hot Foot   Use Devil Be Gone.
Hummingbird   Use Passion.

I Can/You Can't   Use Controlling.
Impossible Objective   Use Helping Hand.
Indian Guide   Use Spirit Guide.
Influence   Use Compelling.
Invisible   Use Mystic Veil.
Jalap/Jalop   Use High John the Conqueror.
Judge Be for Me   Use Just Judge.
Jury Winning   Use Black Candle Tobacco.
Keep Away Enemies   Use Protection.
Keep Away Evil   Use Devil's Trap.
Keep Me   Combine Midas and Bending.
La Flamme   Use Aphrodisia.
Law Stay Away   Combine Mystic Veil, Van Van, and Black Candle
   Tobacco.
Life   Use New Life.
Lodestone   Use Talisman.
Look Me Over   Use Attraction.
Lost and Away   Use Devil Be Gone.
Lottery   Combine Lucky Hand, Talisman, and Midas.
Love Me   Combine Come to Me and Lovers.
Lucky Business   Better Business.
Lucky Dice   Use Lucky Hand.
Lucky Lodestone   Use Talisman.
Lucky Mojo   Use Talisman.
Lucky Lottery   Combine Lucky Hand, Talisman, and Midas.
Lucky Mystic   Use Psychic.
Lucky Number   Combine Lucky Hand, Talisman, and Midas.
Lucky Prophet   Use Vision.
Lucky Seven   Combine Luck and Seven Powers.
Magic Carpet   Use Astral Projection.
Master Key   Use King Solomon.
Mimosa Magic   Use Magick.
Millionaire   Combine King Solomon and Midas.
Mind Bender   Use Bending.
Mint Bouquet   Use Jinx Removing.

Miracle   Use Rose Cross.
Mistletoe   Use Better Business.
My Desire   Use Aphrodisia.
My Man   Use India Bouquet.
New Money   Combine New Life and Money Drawing.
No Hex   Use Uncrossing.
Parting   Use New Life.
Pax   Use Peace.
Pay Me   Combine Controlling and Snake.
Peace and Protection   Use House Blessing.
Peony   Use Better Business.
Prayer   Use Meditation.
Queen   Use Sheba.
Repentance   Use New Life.
Repelling   Use Devil Be Gone.
Rose of Crucifixion   Use Rose Cross.
Run Devil Run   Use Devil's Trap.
Sacred   Use Temple of Light.
St. Alexander   Use Protection.
St. Anthony   Use Frankincense.
St. Barbara   Use Healing.
St. Christopher   Use Temple of Light.
St. Expidus   Use Myrrh.
St. Ignatius   Use Angel.
St. Joseph   Use High John the Conqueror.
St. Jude   Use Special Favors.
St. Michael   Use Seven Powers.
St. Peter   Use Banishing.
San Cipriano   Use Vision.
San Jacob   Use Bayberry.
San Ramon   Use Midas.
Sanctuary   Use Temple of Light.
Santa Clara   Combine Protection, Dragon's Blood, and Protection
   from Thieves.
Sensation   Use Fantasy.

Sesame   Use Holy Smoke.
Separation   Use Banishing.
Seven Circle   Use Seven Powers.
Shifting Sands   Use New Life.
Showers of Gold   Use Midas.
Song of Solomon   Use King Solomon.
Special Dice   Use Lucky Hand.
Spiritualist   Use Mystic Veil.
Squint   Use India Bouquet.
Sure to Win   Use Lucky Hand.
Swallow's Blood   Use Dragon's Blood.
Swallow's Eye   Use Dove's Flight.
Swallow's Heart   Use Dove's Flight.
Tame   Use Peace.
Teasing Lover   Use Lovers.
Temple   Use Temple of Light.
Three Jacks   Use Lucky Hand.
Three Jacks and a King   Combine Lucky Hand with High John
   the Conqueror.
Touch Me Not   Use Banishing.
Tranquil   Combine Peace and Tranquility.
Triumph   Use High John the Conqueror.
Turn Back   Use Criss Cross.
Turquoise   Use Easy Life.
Twisting   Use Criss Cross.
Unbinding   Use Uncrossing.
Unfaithful   Use India Bouquet.
Unhexing   Use Uncrossing.
Untruthful   Use Moonlight.
Vibration   Use Jezebel.
Victory   Use High John the Conqueror.
Wealthy Way   Combine Success and Money Drawing.
Weed of Misfortune   Use Jinx Remover.
Will Power   Use Controlling.
Winning Circle   Use Lucky Hand.

Wisdom   Use Witch.
Wishbone   Use Wishing.
Wolf's Blood   Use Wolfsong.
Wolf's Heart   Use Wolfsong.
XYZ   Combine Witch with Protection.
Zobra   Use Psychic.

THE ATTUNEMENT

7

The Tree of Life bears the leaves,
With thirty-two steps to receive.
Ancient mystics of days of old,
Share the wisdom of the gold.
A gentle touch to wake the soul,
Words of wisdom to sight the goal.
Color the earth with the rhyme,
Heal the people one at a time.

BELLADONNA

The Chakras

A chakra is a source of energy that exists in the realm of psychic and spiritual power. It is invisible, but gifted clairvoyants are able to see these chakras clearly. Seven main chakras lie along the spinal column in the human body. Hundreds of minor chakras are located mainly in the hands and feet. Due to physical, spiritual, and emotional issues, chakras can easily become misaligned and out of tune, causing disharmony of the spirit.

Each chakra has a specific color and energy. Chakras are shaped like little spoked wheels whirling at various speeds as they process energy. Each chakra is connected to the others by way of the nadis, which are channels of subtle energy.

Each chakra has a specific number of spokes and speed of vibration. When chakras are balanced and healthy, their colors are sharp and luminous. Their rotations are smooth and even. When a person is in poor physical or emotional health, the chakras become cloudy, irregular, and sluggish in their movement.

Individuals who do body work, such as massage therapists, Reiki therapists, healers of therapeutic touch, and so forth, are all able to align the chakras of other people. The medical world is beginning to recognize that chakras really do exist, even though they cannot be seen. Some clairvoyants have the power to align the chakras for others, but a person who does hands-on body work has an advantage over them. Each person can learn to align his or her own chakras.

Chakra Number One   The primary color is red and it has four spokes. It is located at the base of the spine. Its concern is with self-preservation, one's animal nature, taste, and smell. It is the least complex of the seven major chakras.

Chakra Number Two   The primary color is orange and it has six spokes. It is located near the genitals and the reproductive organs. Its concern is with digestion and the liver, pancreas, and spleen.

Chakra Number Three   The primary color is yellow and it has ten spokes. It is located between the solar plexus and the navel. Its concern is the emotions and the adrenal glands, pancreas, liver, and stomach.

Chakra Number Four   The primary color is pink and it has twelve glowing golden spokes. It is located between the shoulder blades in the center of the chest. Its concern is the thymus gland, and it influences the immune system. It is also linked to the higher consciousness and unconditional love.

Chakra Number Five   The primary color is blue and it has sixteen spokes. It is located in the throat. Its concern is the thyroid and parathyroid glands, self-expression, expanded consciousness, and the search for truth.

Chakra Number Six   The primary color is purple and it has ninety-six spokes. It is located between the brows at the location of the third eye. Its concern is the pituitary gland, pineal gland, psychic sense, spiritual enlightenment, intelligence, and all psychic powers.

Chakra Number Seven   The primary color is white and it has 972 glowing white spokes. It is located at the top of the head. Its concern is conscious evolution. This chakra will bring supreme enlightenment.

To align your own chakras, visualize the appropriate color at the correct location in your body. Then visualize each chakra spinning like a spoked wheel. At some point in your visualization, see all seven colors aligned. Once you can see the alignment, place an invisible cord between your first and seventh chakras and attach this cord into the earth. Not only will your chakras be aligned, but you will also be grounded to do any type of spiritual work.

THE SEVEN CHAKRAS

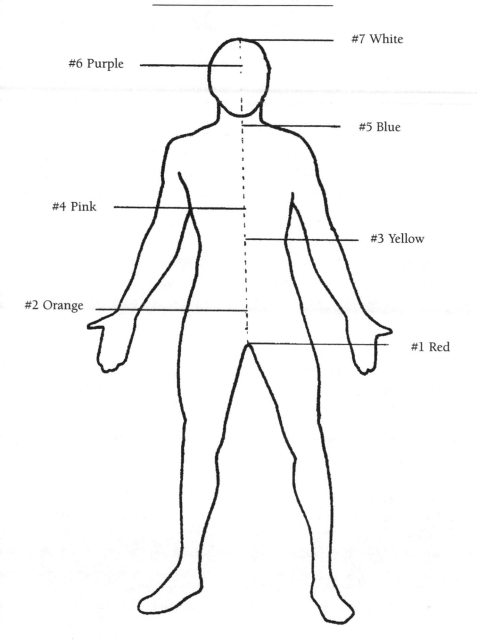

Healings

In ancient times the Wiccans were known as healers and midwives. Wiccans relied heavily upon herbs to be their medicine. They practiced healing using every aspect of medicine, from ingestion to poultices. The majority of practicing Wiccans were females. As with all professions, some people were more naturally inclined than others to be healers. Over time, as science and modern allopathic medicine became more socially accepted, there was less demand for herbal healing and people's secrets and talents in these areas waned greatly.

Several different methods are used by natural healers to invoke the healing process. All natural healers know the Goddess and the God are the true healers and with the approval of the Deities, the natural healers have been chosen to administer the channel of healing. They use no drugs whatsoever. A few of the methods of natural healing are faith healing, therapeutic touch, Reiki, or sensory healing. Whatever the method used, all healers agree that they process and transmit positive energy coming from the Divine Source. They perform a body scan for the affliction and direct the Divine Light into the area needing to be healed. All natural healers agree that a healing will not work if the patient is negative, fearful, distrustful, or filled with guilt or hate. Children are the easiest patients to heal because they do not usually possess the negative qualities of adults. If the patient's heart is closed, then the powers of the Goddess and God will not be received, but if the patient's heart is pure, then all of the blessings from the Goddess and the God will be opened to that person, if this is what the Deities choose. Many pure-hearted individuals have passed away due to illness. It is my belief these people have worked out their karmic areas for this lifetime and they have earned the privilege of a direct path to the Kingdom of Heaven.

Jesus is the best-known healer in history. Some people choose not to believe that Jesus was anything but a man. In my opinion, he is the son of the Goddess and God and therefore had divine intervention to help with healing. The love and compassion Jesus had for mankind are two of the requirements a natural healer must have. A true healer has great compassion for the afflicted. Without compassion, the positive Light cannot flow through. The afflicted does not have to be of a specific religion or belief to be healed, but the afflicted must have a positive attitude that anything is possible.

Most natural healers have had some sort of experience with clairvoyance or another psychic gift before they discovered their ability to heal. Most healers have practiced or learned other methods, but they stay with whatever method feels comfortable and positive for them. Healers will never promise results. If they do, then they are not truly healers. Only the Goddess and the God can promise and deliver results. The healer can only promise a sincere effort to transmit the healing.

Edgar Cayce was one of the best and most well-documented psychic healers of the twentieth century. During his healing sessions, he put himself into a very deep trance and was able to separate his energy body from his physical body. During this trance-like state, he was able to communicate verbally while his energy body seemed to merge internally into the patient. He was able to psychically see the ailment and then prescribe what the patient needed. He talked in a monotone voice while in his trance. His wife recorded the sessions so nothing would be missed or left out. After his trance had started, he would say, "We are now with the patient." Who were "we"? The only "we" it ever could be—the Angels. Through Edgar Cayce, many healings occurred. He always remained an honest and sincere healer, even though his fame was great. Many people argue that Edgar Cayce was only a channeler—but through his channeling, miracles of healing occurred.

As everyone has some psychic gifts, many also have the gift of healing. Through practice and by channeling the Light energy, people can use this gift to cure and even save lives. As with all talents, practice can perfect a method of healing. The subject can be as simple as a cat or as challenging as a cancer victim. The healer needs to open her own chakras before the healing can begin, summon the Angels and Good Spirits to aid in all healing areas, ask the Goddess and the God for healing to be transmitted, and then proceed. Whatever the method used, ask for Divine Healing. When the healing session is over, it is absolutely vital to shake off all absorbed energies from the healing. If this is not done, the healer may soon become the subject with the same illness.

How to Do a Body Scan and Administer a Healing

The Body Scan

1. Align your chakras.

2. Pray to the Goddess and God for the subject to be open to the healing. Ask the Angels and the Good Spirits to be with you and aid you in your scanning and also in your process of channeling the Light energy.

3. Erase all preconceived diagnoses and information you have obtained regarding the subject.

4. Have your subject lie completely flat on his back, comforted with a pillow and blanket if necessary.

5. Instruct the subject to relax and visualize a summer day, lying in a hammock, completely relaxed.

6. Warm the energy of your hands by rubbing them together vigorously. Start at the subject's feet.

7. Close your eyes and scan upward toward the first chakra area of the subject. Feel for a magnetic pull that will alert you to an afflicted area. At the first chakra, open your eyes and see if the chakra is aligned. Move to the second chakra, and so on. This scanning process should take about two to five minutes.

8. Make mental notes as to which chakras are not aligned and which areas have a strong magnetic pull.

9. Start at the seventh chakra and work downward toward the subject's feet with the same scanning process.

10. Have the subject roll over onto his stomach and start the same scanning process, beginning with the feet and continuing to the top of the head.

The Healing

1. Pray to the Goddess and God for the healing Light energy to flow from your hands and into the afflicted areas of the subject. Tell the subject to lie on his back.

2. Tell the subject to visualize a powerful waterspout shooting up through his feet and out the top of his head.

3. Warm the energy in your hands by rubbing them together vigorously. Begin at the subject's feet. Work with your hands approximately one inch above the subject's body.

4. There will be a sensation of heat rushing from your hands into the afflicted areas. The area that is afflicted should be Lighted for as long as you feel the pull of heat from your hands. When the heat dissipates, move on to the next area. Do not speak to the subject until the entire process is complete.

5. Areas of the body that have been surgically removed or that have irreparable scar tissue, will feel cold or void.

6. Continue moving up toward the head area. When approaching the chakra areas, visualize the chakra having the appropriate color and whirling at a healthy speed.

7. When you have reached the crown chakra and the energy has dissipated, tell the subject to turn over onto his stomach. Begin the process again, starting at the feet.

8. Remember to allow the Light energy enough time at each afflicted area. Your hands will tell you when it is time to move on.

9. After you end at the subject's crown chakra, clap your hands and shake them vigorously to shake off all excess illness. While you were depositing Light energy, your body absorbed the pain or illness. It localizes in the hands and will spread throughout your body if it is not shaken off.

10. It is rare to have a recovery after the first healing. Tell the subject to drink at least ten eight-ounce glasses of water per day for the next two days, to flush impurities out of the body. You

and your subject will both feel extremely tired after the healing. Tell the subject what afflicted areas you sensed. The subject will confirm or deny these areas. If pain is prominent
when the healing begins, the pain should be either greatly less-
ened or nonexistent by the end of the session. The subject will
express feelings of heat or tingling after you have worked on
certain areas. Plenty of rest and flushing with water will greatly
improve the body's healing. It is not recommended to undergo
more than one healing per day.

Qabala

The Qabala can be spelled several different ways, including Kab-
balah, Caballah, Caballa, and Cabala. The Qabala is a Hebrew word
meaning "that which is received." The Qabala is an oracle from
which to receive enlightenment from the supreme source of the
Goddess and the God.

The Qabala is based on the fourth branch of Judaism. It is both
an ancient and a modern system of divine communication. Though
it dates prior to the medieval era, it became more popular in
medieval times. The Qabala is based upon the Jewish Torah and was
used as a tool to speak to God. In modern paganism, we refer to the
Qabala as the tool to speak to the Goddess and the God.

The Qabala is a secret oral tradition passed down from teacher to
student. The only ones who were taught this method of communication were the Jewish people and the Witches. These two
groups actually conspired and aided each other during times of
persecution.

Even though the Qabala is based upon the Torah, other Jewish
scriptures and sacred literature were used. The Qabala is not a dis-
ciplinary table of dos and don'ts, but rather a method of how to
achieve enlightenment and union with the Goddess and God in our
everyday lives.

According to the legend, the God taught the Qabala to the
Angels. The Angels taught it to Adam in order to provide mankind

a pathway back to the God. The descendants of Adam taught the Qabala to Noah. From Noah it was passed to Abraham and from Abraham it was passed to Moses. From Moses it was passed to seventy elders he initiated.

The Merkabah Mystics, who flourished from 1000 B.C. to 100 A.D., believed the entire goal of man was to reach the Throne World. The Throne World is what they believed to be Heaven and the vehicle to the Throne World was a chariot. Their belief was founded on Elijah exiting the world by way of a chariot (a story found in the Old Testament). In order to enter the Throne World, a person had to pass through the seven Heavenly Mansions. This is where the theory of heaven having many levels is founded. The lower levels of Heaven are the learning levels and the higher levels of Heaven are closer to the Goddess and God. It is believed that beings on the lower levels of Heaven are taught the Qabala. If people study and learn the Qabala here on earth, then their passage out of this world will automatically place them in a higher level of Heaven and thus closer to the Goddess and the God.

The Qabala is based upon a spiritual map called the Tree of Life. The Tree of Life is made up of ten Sephiroth. The Sephiroth are the spiritual laws we need to learn. It is said that only the most stable and purest of heart are permitted to approach the Tree of Life. The lower seven Sephiroth correspond to the seven chakras. The upper three Sephiroth are the mystical steps toward unity with the Goddess and the God.

The Qabala has a total of thirty-two secret paths to wisdom and communication with the Goddess and God. The twenty-two paths correspond to the twenty-two letters of the Hebrew alphabet and also to the twenty-two major arcana in the tarot deck.

When you meditate using the Tree of Life, visualize each Sephiroth with its own vibrating color. Moving forward into the other twenty-two steps, visualize the picture of the tarot card, and then visualize the letter of the Hebrew alphabet with which it corresponds over the top of the image. Each person who studies the Qabala will have different experiences. There is no right or wrong way. The Goddess and God will let you know if you're on the right path.

Keep a journal of the knowledge you obtain from the Qabala; it is a wonderful experience. It is also an amazing process of growth and communication at the highest level.

The Qabala is one of the first resources that inspired the theory of the transmigration of souls, or reincarnation.

Do not be surprised if the Goddess and God actually reveal their names to you. It has happened before.

The Tree of Life

1. MALKUTH—Kingdom—Black

   Awakens the greater common sense. Helps to overcome greed and laziness. Tapping into this knowledge creates greater physical strength and energy. At this level you can see your Guardian Angel.

2. YESOD—Foundation—Violet

   Awakens psychic energy and intuition. Helps to stimulate dreams and independence. Tapping into this knowledge creates the ability to overcome idleness and impulsiveness. This Sephiroth opens emotional balance.

3. HOD—Glory—Orange

   Awakens inspiration, idealism, warmth, and unselfishness. Tapping into this knowledge creates the ability to overcome lust, jealousy, and emotional upsets. This level can open the kingdom of nature.

4. NISAH—Victory—Green

   Awakens nature, fertility, harmony, and the equilibrium. Tapping into this knowledge creates the ability to protect the instincts and intuition. This Sephiroth opens all of the emotions.

5. TIPHAR—Beauty—Yellow

Awakens the Christ consciousness, healing, and compassion. Tapping into this knowledge creates the process of overcoming fears, insecurity, and false pride. The Keeper of the Holy Grail can be seen here.

6. GEBURAH—Severity and Strength—Red

Awakens courage, strength, and the ability to slay dragons. Tapping into this knowledge creates the ability to overcome anger, fear, timidness, and aggression. This opens the ability to have better judgment.

7. CHESED—Mercy—Blue

Awakens peace, devotion, and abundance. Tapping into this knowledge creates the ability to overcome stinginess, self-righteousness, and hypocrisy. This level protects all teachers with the winds of mercy.

8. BINAH—Understanding—Brownish Black

Awakens a greater understanding for all things. This is the level at which we learn why we made the sacrifices that we have. Tapping into this knowledge creates the ability to promote a higher intuition and helps us to understand the processes of birth and death. This level is where devotion and healing will occur.

9. CHOKMA—Wisdom—Gray

Awakens greater initiative, inspiration, and vision. It is the realization of one's hidden abilities. Tapping into this knowledge creates the ability to overcome forgetfulness and inefficiency. This level enables you to manifest all desires.

10. KETHER—Crown—White

Awakens our humanity through an evolutionary process. Helps to amplify and intensify any aspect of life. Tapping into this knowledge creates the power of transformation. It also helps to overcome illusion, self-denial, and negative imagery.

THE TREE OF LIFE

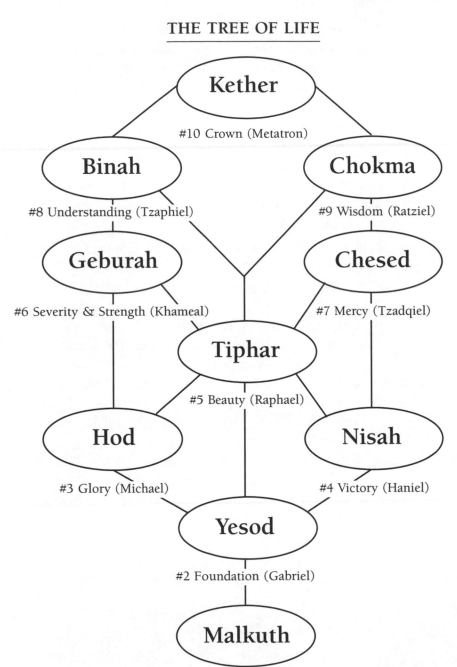

Kether

#10 Crown (Metatron)

Binah

Chokma

#8 Understanding (Tzaphiel)

#9 Wisdom (Ratziel)

Geburah

Chesed

#6 Severity & Strength (Khameal)

#7 Mercy (Tzadqiel)

Tiphar

#5 Beauty (Raphael)

Hod

Nisah

#3 Glory (Michael)

#4 Victory (Haniel)

Yesod

#2 Foundation (Gabriel)

Malkuth

#1 Kingdom (Sandalphon)

THE TWENTY-TWO STEPS

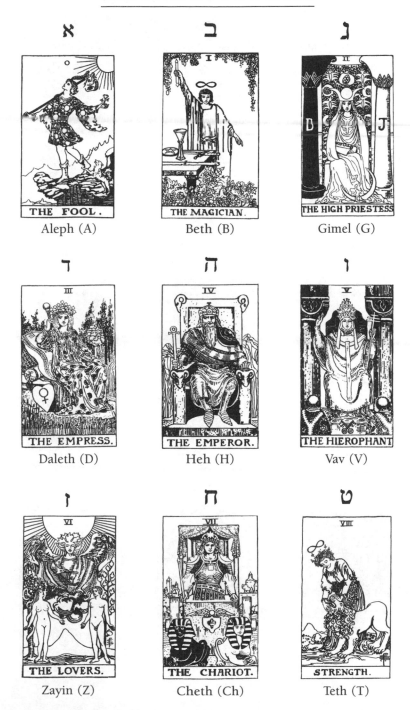

א
THE FOOL.
Aleph (A)

ב
THE MAGICIAN.
Beth (B)

ג
THE HIGH PRIESTESS
Gimel (G)

ד
THE EMPRESS.
Daleth (D)

ה
THE EMPEROR.
Heh (H)

ו
THE HIEROPHANT
Vav (V)

ז
THE LOVERS.
Zayin (Z)

ח
THE CHARIOT.
Cheth (Ch)

ט
STRENGTH.
Teth (T)

Yod (Y)

Kaph (K)

Lamed (L)

Mem (M)

Nun (N)

Samekh (S)

Ayin (O)

Peh (P)

Tsaddi (Ts)

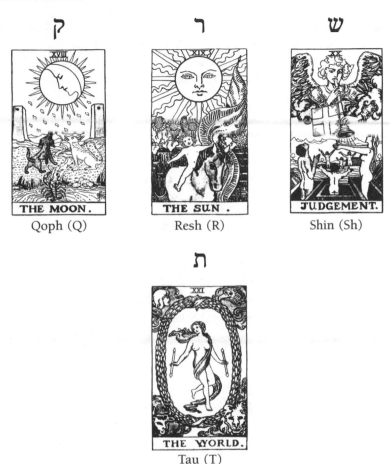

ק

ר

ש

THE MOON.
Qoph (Q)

THE SUN .
Resh (R)

JUDGEMENT.
Shin (Sh)

ת

THE WORLD.
Tau (T)

Aura

An aura is an envelope of vital energy that radiates from everything and every person in nature. An aura is not visible by natural vision, but is visible by clairvoyance. The aura appears as a halo of light or a multicolored mist fading off into space. An aura has no boundaries, but it does appear to have sparks, rays, and streamers. Because an aura is invisible, the question is raised as to how the clairvoyant picks up the color spectrum. Apparently, a magnetic field will register as colored light to the clairvoyant. Using the thirteen colors with their magickal potential, it is easy for the clairvoyant to pick up a person's mood. It is also easy to see what motivates certain individuals. The color of their aura will reveal everything.

For instance, if people appear to have a soft blue cast around them, this means their mood is passive and tranquil. If people are glowing pink, they have a feeling of love around them. If someone has a gold aura that radiates bright streamers, it would probably be a person who is closing a business deal.

Astral Projection

Astral projection is the practice of projecting the energy body away from the physical body. It is, in a sense, the ability to separate the soul from the physical body. Astral projection is also referred to as an out-of-body experience. The energy body is connected to the physical body by way of a silver cord. This silver cord stays completely attached to both bodies until the time of death. At that time, the cord simply snaps in half and the energy body then travels to its destination.

An out-of-body experience usually occurs when one is sleeping, daydreaming, or in meditation. It is something that can be practiced and perfected to occur at will.

One lesson we learn from the experience of astral projection is realizing that the soul and the body are two different entities and that they really do separate. The soul has a destination when the body dies. An advantage of astral projection is being able to visit places and people without ever leaving your home.

During an experience of astral projection, you can actually see and sense your surroundings. Verbal communication is the only aspect lacking. Time seems to stand still. When you return to your physical body, there is a body slam. It is not painful, but it is rather startling. This is similar to when we "jump awake." When you make a conscious effort to astrally project, there is a color method used to separate the energy body from the physical body.

Seven Steps to Astral Projection

1. Be completely relaxed, focused, and quiet.

2. Open and align all seven chakras.

3. Meditate upon your destination. Do meditative breathing.

4. Surround yourself with a blue aura.

5. Do the rainbow method of colors: visualize red, then orange, yellow, green, blue, indigo, and finally violet.

6. Lift out of the body and seek your destination.

7. Be aware of your surroundings.

To return to your physical body, simply reverse the rainbow. Visualize violet, then indigo, blue, green, yellow, orange, and finally red.

While you are experiencing astral projection, observe the silver cord attached to the energy body. Your physical body will experience slow, rhythmic breathing and a feeling of temporary paralysis, while your soul experiences the most wonderful feeling of flying. Enjoy!

8

DIVINING

Spread the cards and Runes be cast,
Know your future and your past.
Gaze the ball and roll the dice,
Do it once and do it twice.
Pendulum swings and talking boards,
Reveal the truth like a cutting sword.
See them all as a positive sign,
To know them all is to divine.

BELLADONNA

D ivining is the ancient art of foretelling the future. An oracle is a tool with which we divine. Hundreds of methods are used to divine and there are hundreds of different types of oracles. Divining has been frequently associated with Witchcraft and sorcery, but even those outside the religion of Wicca are able to divine.

In the Old Testament, the word *diviner* was translated as *Witch*. By the first century A.D., Witchcraft had a bad reputation and not long after that, Witchcraft was deemed illegal and punishable by law. The penalties for Witchcraft varied from public humiliation and a fine to the death sentence. In spite of the law, Witches and Prophets still survived, along with their tools for divining.

A good Witch will have at least one solid method in which to divine, if not several. The Witch may feel more comfortable with her own natural gifts of clairvoyance and intuition as her method of divining, but she needs to be at least familiar with other methods and tools used in divining. The hardest person the diviner will ever read is the diviner herself.

The session in which a person divines is called a reading. The reader is the diviner and the person receiving the reading is called the seeker.

In this chapter we will cover six different methods of divining: dreams, tarot cards, divining yes or no, pendulum, crystal ball or magical mirror, and runes.

It is important to note that when reading other people without their permission, you stand at the threshold of invading their privacy. In many readings you may discover secret fantasies, the skeletons in their closet, and also other people's undisclosed thoughts. The invasion of privacy opens the reader to the same consequence— the invasion of her privacy. If this is acceptable to you, also consider that the information may be more than you would truly like to know. For example, you are reading about your husband-to-be and you stumble across a secret fantasy he has about your sister or a close friend. Do you judge him? Do you no longer want to marry him for fear that his fantasy may become a reality? Are you so jealous that you keep some distance between your sister or friend, who have no idea of what is going on? The answer is simple: Do not tread into any areas you are unable to accept without maturity, prejudice, or passion. You are not a judge, you are just a reader. Fantasies are fantasies. If you were to examine your own heart, are there any secret fantasies you have about other people? Of course, there are. We all have them. We do not always want fantasies to become reality. The question then arises, how does the reader know the difference between fantasy and reality in the reading? A skilled reader will know how to ask the Guides to identify the difference. The Guides are the Good Angels and Good Spirits who aid us in our everyday lives. Without the Guides to influence the reading, we would be guessing and playing games instead of divining.

All methods of divining are controlled by the Goddess and God. The Guides are our go-betweens. Our Guides will usually talk to us very simply and without complexity. When divining, the little voice in your head is usually a Good Spirit. It is irrelevant to ask your Guide its name or any other useless information. A good reader will always ask the Guides to help her before the reading even begins. The Guides will flow through the reader, not the seeker. If the seeker wants to know the name of the cocker spaniel she used to have, the Guides will probably decline to answer at all. The Guides truly have better things to do than to play mind games with curiosity seekers. Intuition is the only thing the reader can rely on if the questions are not serious enough for the Guides to help. There are two types of seekers: serious people who need spiritual help and the curious who do this for fun. A good reader can accept both types of clients as long as this is identified from the start. The Guides will rarely tolerate the curious.

Two things that make divining impossible: fear and a reader who does not have purity of heart.

If you are pregnant or nursing a baby, all of your psychic abilities are being transmitted to your baby. Divining is practically impossible during this time and it is highly recommended that someone else do the divining for you until this natal time has passed.

The fee for divining or reading for someone may vary from a trade of service to $200. The important thing to remember is never to offer free readings and never read without some sort of exchange being discussed first. The exception to this rule is when the Witch is learning how to read. It may take a year of learning before the Witch is highly accurate. Recording the readings is recommended during your learning process. The reason for charging is that this is in the best interest of the seeker. Remember, the Universe operates on an exchange system. For ten years I conducted readings without charging. I always felt that they should come from the heart and not be for profit. By the end of the ten years it was overwhelming to discover that I had become poor and weary, and the clients had had unusual ranges of bad luck. The clients had not taken the advice very seriously, and only the bad parts of their readings were coming true. When I started charging for readings, the lives of my clients improved and changed for the better. The advice was heeded and the negative aspects were all avoided. I have done readings in exchange for alfalfa sprouts and Mexican cooking lessons. Any type of exchange will do. If there is no exchange, you are denying your client a positive future.

On the average, the Wiccan reader will have a 75 to 88 percent accuracy rate. The remaining 12 to 25 percent is left up to the Goddess and God, and the free-will margin the client retains.

The following methods of divining are from age-old practices that are still strong, positive, and magickal today.

Tarot

The exact year that tarot cards were invented is not clear. Many experts believe they came into existence before the fourteenth century. The Italians seem to be their originators.

The playing-card deck of fifty-two cards is based on the tarot. The cards of the major arcana were deleted from the deck and the knights and pages were combined into jacks. The four suits derive from wands (clubs), swords (spades), cups (hearts), and pentacles (diamonds).

The Renaissance nobility used tarot cards in divining their futures. They relied heavily upon their tarot for weekly consultation. Others used tarot as a game of amusement.

The occult applications of tarot became popular in Europe during the late eighteenth century. Since that time the tarot has been used in various methods of divination.

Presently, tarot is a popular choice to use as a tool or channel to determine events of the past, present, and future. The reader must also possess an unbiased mind and purity of heart when asking for answers. As always, free will can intercept anything and the future can always be altered.

The Major Arcana

The major arcana contains highly spiritual cards, dealing with messages from the Divine. There are twenty-two in total and they represent God's will and fate. If four or more are represented in a ten-card layout, then this fate is likely to happen exactly as laid out. If this is a positive aspect, then let fate ride. If it is negative, then change these events so that something more positive can occur. The fate is in your own hands.

The Minor Arcana

Fifty-six cards, including the sixteen court cards, make up the minor arcana. The court cards represent people and also some events. The forty remaining minor arcana cards deal with earthly occurrences—triumphs, battles, money, love, and so forth.

The minor arcana has four suits: wands, swords, cups and pentacles. They are numbered from one through ten. Aces represent the number one.

The Format

Of the seventy-eight cards in a deck, only ten are used in each layout. Only one question should be asked per layout. The cards are positioned in what is known as the Celtic Cross. Cards one through six actually resemble a cross. Cards seven through ten are in a vertical line.

As you shuffle, concentrate on the exact question. Your wording should be precise. After you feel that you have the appropriate answer, use your power hand (i.e., your non-dominant hand) to cut the cards into three stacks to the left. Restack the cards from right to left so that they are back in one stack.

The deck should be placed so that the cards are upright to you and when they are dealt, they will be right-side up. They should not be mixed (some upside down and some right-side up.) It is not necessary to read the in-reverse method to get exact answers.

Now you are ready for the layout:

Card no. 1   is placed first. This position represents the *issue* of the question.

Card no. 2   is placed directly below card no. 1 and this position represents what *opposes the issue,* for better or worse.

Card no. 3   is placed directly below card no. 2 and this card represents the heart or the *base of the question.*

Card no. 4   is placed to the left of card no. 1. This position represents what has *already happened* or taken place.

Card no. 5   is placed directly above card no. 1. This position represents the *possible future.*

Card no. 6   is placed directly to the right side of card no. 1. This position represents the *immediate future.*

Now look at the six cards you have placed. You can see how the layout resembles a cross.

Card no. 7   is placed in a vertical column to the right side of card
no. 3. This position represents *the concern.*

Card no. 8   is placed directly above card no. 7 and is to the right
side of card no. 2. This position represents the *reflection of
family or friends.*

Card no. 9   is placed directly above card no. 8 and is to the right
side of card no. 1. This position represents the *hoped-for or
hoped-against scenario.*

Card no. 10   is placed directly above card no. 9 and is to the
right side of card no. 5. This position represents the *outcome of
the question.*

THE CELTIC CROSS METHOD

5			10
4	1	6	9.
	2		8
	3		7

The Major Arcana

0 *The Fool* Visualize a young court jester. This card also brings to mind a simple child with genius talents. Purity of heart; self-knowledge; intuition and wisdom. It can also advise caution against being foolish.

1 *The Magician* Visualize a powerful man in ritualistic garments. He has four tools on his altar: a sword, a cup, a pentacle, and a wand. His hand extends upward as if reaching for the highest power to aid him. The harnessing of energy and turning it into a force. With wisdom and mastery any magical plan can be put into motion for a positive result. It can also advise caution against trickery.

2 *The High Priestess* Visualize a sacred, ritualistic-looking female. She wears an elaborate headdress and a cross around her neck. The unknown woman; a woman in the shadows; she may also have penetrating intuition and foresight. Her description is a mystery.

3 *The Empress* Visualize a matronly female, warm, smiling, and beautiful. She appears goddesslike and wears a laurel wreath on her head. She nurtures all that she touches. Motherly, Mother Nature, a pregnant female. She is warm and devoted to her family and manifests a great deal of feminine intuition.

4 *The Emperor* Visualize a very important legislative-type of man. He is a superior and holds a crystal in his left hand. He wears a laurel crown and flowing robes. A wise man with great authority; a King Solomon–type. He is usually older than middle-aged and he bears a title such as father, doctor, lawyer, and so forth.

5 *The Hierophant* Visualize an elderly male who appears to be deeply involved with a church. He looks like an ancient priest or church official. A religious ceremony or rite, such as a wedding or funeral. It is a gathering of people for spiritual work. It can also mean to conform to the public's view.

6 *The Lovers*   Visualize an Adam-and-Eve–type couple. The
   perfect male and the perfect female. They are extremely
   beautiful and usually nude. True, pure love; intimate and
   trusting; it shows sexual attraction and physical love. This
   love is unconditional.

7 *The Chariot*   Visualize a well-adorned soldier or hero who is
   parading victoriously in a well-decorated chariot. He is proud
   and exalted in a crowd of townspeople. Victory over life's
   opposing forces; this shows a luxurious lifestyle. It represents
   earned wealth and high social status, accomplishment, and
   recognition.

8 *Strength*   Visualize a beautiful maiden who fondly caresses a
   male lion. The beauty and the beast. She strokes the massive,
   gentle lion with kindness. Courage; compassion and
   determination; also, emotional and inner strength.

9 *The Hermit*   Visualize an ancient man with a long white
   beard and wearing flowing robes. His left hand holds a staff
   and his right hand holds a brilliant beacon that illuminates a
   great path. Inside his lantern is the divine star. Divine
   counsel; great vision and infinite wisdom from the heavens;
   the divine light is shining on the correct path.

10 *Wheel of Fortune*   Visualize a gambling wheel. It seems to be
   in perpetual motion and is also somewhat tilted. Fate in
   turning motion; a gamble; luck; possible gain.

11 *Justice*   adorned in red and the scales of justice balance
   before him. Legal papers in process; a possible court
   appearance; legalities in any form.

12 *The Hanged Man*   Visualize a man who is suspended in air
   upside down by way of a gallows. Sudden reversal in a
   situation; major changes; suspension of time; a 180-degree
   turn.

13 *Death*   Visualize a full skeleton. He is holding a flag of death
   and is riding upon a horse. Change; the birth of a new idea; a
   physical birth; transformation.

14 *Temperance* Visualize a beautiful winged Angel. She is holding two urns and is pouring a liquid from one into the other. Patience; accomplishment through self-control; harmony.

15 *Devil* Visualize a black, horned demon. He is evil and foreboding on sight. Destruction; black magic; deceit; negativity.

16 *The Tower* Visualize a tall, black tower. It has been struck by lightning and has a fire within. Two people are falling from the tower. Abandonment; the destruction of a relationship; having to leave one's home; severe disruption.

17 *The Star* Visualize a young maiden by a stream of water. From her hands pour the waters of life. A brilliant star is behind her. Success; bright outlook on projects; completion in positive respects; satisfaction and accomplishment.

18 *The Moon* Visualize the full moon on a dark night. A dog and a wolf sit upon a mountain top howling at the moon. Psychic abilities; an unknown present; be wary of what is not sensed. Proceed with extreme caution.

19 *The Sun* Visualize a smiling child riding on a pony. The sun is beaming and giving life to all it touches. Happiness; good health; sincerity; success; love abounds.

20 *Judgment* Visualize an Angel blowing a trumpet. Graves are opened for the dead to rise. Judgment Day. Rebirth; spiritual awakening; repentance; new beginning; the opening of one's eyes to truth.

21 *The World* Visualize the earth. A female figure stands beneath it. This is the most blessed card in the deck. Perfection; success; the final goal; God's will and blessing are with you.

The Court Cards

There are four suits in the deck: wands, swords, cups, and pentacles. There are also four court cards in each suit: kings, queens, knights, and pages. All together, there are sixteen court cards. The court cards identify people in the reading.

The Swords   The King, Queen, Knight, and Page of Swords all have brownish or dark hair with dark or hazel eyes. This is their outward appearance. If this physical description does not match the person, then the personality profile will fit.

The King of Swords   Visualize a man on a throne with flowing garments. The King of Swords is a determined, active man. He is self-controlled and highly analytical. He has many ideas and desires.

The Queen of Swords   Visualize a queen upon a throne, who is holding one sword. The Queen of Swords is a sharp woman. She is keen and perceptive. She may be lonely or sad. There is a sterile feeling about her.

The Knight of Swords   Visualize a young man in swift battle on his horse. The Knight of Swords has two different meanings (the reader must determine which meaning fits): first, a young or teenaged male who is a defender of rights; second, an interruption in time or events.

The Page of Swords   Visualize a youth holding onto one sword. The Page of Swords has two different meanings (the reader must determine which meaning fits): first, a male or female child; second, bad news may be coming.

The Wands   The King, Queen, Knight, and Page of Wands all are fair-haired people. They are blondes or redheads with light-colored eyes, either blue or green. Their skin is fair. This is their outward appearance. If this physical description does not match the person, then the personality profile will fit.

The King of Wands   Visualize a king who holds one flowering wand as he sits upon his throne. The King of Wands is an honest, mature person. He is devoted and friendly. He is a gentleman. He is usually married and also a father.

The Queen of Wands   Visualize a queen with long, blond hair. The Queen of Wands is sympathetic and understanding. She has charm and grace and is capable of great love. She is a gracious hostess.

The Knight of Wands   Visualize a golden-haired knight sitting on a horse. The Knight of Wands has two different meanings (the reader must determine which meaning fits): first, a young or teenaged male who is capable of being very charming; second, the changing of residence or employment.

The Page of Wands   Visualize a fair-haired youth shouting a message off into the mountains. The Page of Wands has two different meanings (the reader must determine which meaning fits): first, a male or female child; second, good news may be coming.

The Cups   The King, Queen, Knight, and Page of Cups all have brownish hair or dark blond hair with blue or green eyes. This is their outward appearance. If this physical description does not match the person, then the personality profile will fit.

The King of Cups   Visualize a majestic king with full beard and flowing robes. The King of Cups is a responsible person with an easy-flowing attitude. He is generous and intelligent.

The Queen of Cups   Visualize a young, kind face on a beautiful queen who holds a cup in her hands. The Queen of Cups is a warm-hearted, fair-minded person. She is a good mother and is loved and adored.

The Knight of Cups   Visualize a handsome young knight trotting on a horse. He is balancing a cup in his hand. The Knight of Cups has two different meanings (the reader must determine which meaning fits): first, a young or teenaged romantic male; second, a romance is riding into your life.

The Page of Cups   Visualize a young person holding a cup that has a fish coming out of it. The Page of Cups has two different meanings (the reader must determine which meaning fits): first, a male or female child; second, news of birth.

Pentacles   The King, Queen, Knight, and Page of Pentacles all have black or dark hair. They have dark eyes and are not fair-skinned, such as Africans, Asians, Hispanics, and so forth. This is their outward appearance. If this physical description does not match the person, then the personality profile will fit.

The King of Pentacles   Visualize a dark, international-looking man. The King of Pentacles is a wealthy and business-minded male. He is mature and influential.

The Queen of Pentacles   Visualize a dark, prestigious woman with great beauty. The Queen of Pentacles is a wealthy, independent woman. She is knowledgeable and forthright.

The Knight of Pentacles   Visualize a young, dark knight riding a swift black horse. The Knight of Pentacles has two different meanings (the reader must determine which meaning fits): first, a young or teenaged male who controls money; second, the coming of money.

The Page of Pentacles   Visualize a young person holding a pentacle. The Page of Pentacles has two different meanings (the reader must determine which meaning fits): first, a male or female child; second, news of money.

The Suits

Cups   Correspond to hearts. Love and happiness. Pleasures. Emotions. This suit represents passion and deep feelings.

Swords   Correspond to spades. Swords represent courage, strength, and boldness. The suit of leaders and warriors.

Pentacles   Correspond to coins or diamonds. Material and financial matters. Business and occupation. Suit of merchants and tradesmen.

Wands   Correspond to clubs, rods, or batons. Represents growth, progress, and energy. The suit of laborers and workers.

CUPS

Ace of Cups   Visualize a large cup that pours the everflowing waters of life. Cup of Divine Love; the flow of joy and perfection.

Two of Cups   Visualize a man and woman each holding a cup. A promise; engagement; a union or partnership.

Three of Cups   Visualize three young maidens raising three cups in celebration. Time of merriment; celebration; laughter.

Four of Cups   Visualize a young man sitting under a tree with three cups beside him. A heavenly hand extends the fourth cup down to him. A decision is necessary; a new romance may be coming; contemplation.

Five of Cups   Visualize a cloaked figure who seems depressed. Beside him three cups are spilled with two cups left standing. Regrets, partial loss; mourning. Something positive remains, however, even though it cannot be seen at this time.

Six of Cups   Visualize two young children playing with flowers that are held in six cups. Memories; people from the past; childhood.

Seven of Cup   Visualize seven cups suspended in the clouds. Dreams; fantasies; the need to fine-tune ideas to become reality.

Eight of Cups   Visualize eight neatly stacked cups with a cloaked figure leaving them behind. Abandonment or the discontinuance of something; seek higher spiritual ground and leave earthly goods behind.

Nine of Cups   Visualize a plump, happy little man with nine stacked cups behind him. Material attainment; the card of good and plenty; sensual pleasures; more than enough.

Ten of Cups   Visualize a family of four looking upon a rainbow of ten cups. Happiness in the home; good family life; joy; peace; love.

SWORDS

Ace of Swords   Visualize one giant sword. Power; conquest; force.

Two of Swords   Visualize a blindfolded female who holds two swords. Decision between two things; contemplation.

Three of Swords   Visualize a red heart with three swords piercing it. Tears; sorrow; disappointment; despair.

Four of Swords   Visualize four swords that stand alongside a tomb. Illness; time of rest; replenishment; solitude; refrainment.

Five of Swords   Visualize a warrior with three swords in his hand. Two swords remain on the ground. Easy conquest; not much satisfaction in victory; an easy win.

Six of Swords   Visualize a boat transporting passengers and six swords to the opposite shore. Trip or journey; route; a passage away from difficulties.

Seven of Swords   Visualize a warrior carrying five swords and two swords are stuck in the ground behind him. Plan; preparation for things to come; putting priorities in order; being sneaky.

Eight of Swords   Visualize a female who is blindfolded. She is tied and bound with eight swords around her. Stalemate; confusion; restriction; bound.

Nine of Swords   Visualize a woman with her head bowed in despair, crying. There are nine swords above her. Misery; unhappiness; deep worry and despair for either oneself or someone else; stress.

Ten of Swords   Visualize a body lying face down with ten bloody swords in his back. Death; ruin; terrible pain and anguish; total destruction; a bitter finale; possible blood loss.

PENTACLES

Ace of Pentacles   Visualize a large golden pentacle. Prosperity; perfection; gold; bliss; treasures; universal beginning for money.

Two of Pentacles   Visualize a jester juggling two pentacles. Balance; harmony in the midst; yin and yang.

Three of Pentacles   Visualize an apprentice working on a stained glass of three pentacles. The learning of a skill or trade; education; learning to perfect ability; writing abilities.

Four of Pentacles   Visualize a person who is holding on tightly to four pentacles. Hanging on to a situation or to what is valuable; unable to share with others; stinginess.

Five of Pentacles   Visualize two poverty-stricken people in a snowstorm. Five pentacles are above their heads. Poverty; material trouble; loss; failure; destitution; illness.

Six of Pentacles   Visualize a prosperous man with a necklace
of six pentacles. He is weighing money on a scale. A philan-
thropist; the gift of charity; kindness; generosity; a gift is
coming.

Seven of Pentacles   Visualize a man who is resting wearily against
his hoe, looking at a mound of seven pentacles. Hard work;
labor; progress by means of great effort; a job well done.

Eight of Pentacles   Visualize a craftsman who is making eight
pentacles. Employment; craftsmanship at work; a skilled person.

Nine of Pentacles   Visualize a well-dressed woman with a bird
perched on her arm. Nine pentacles surround her. An
independent person; a financially secure person; a person who
is alone; a blessed solitude.

Ten of Pentacles   Visualize a busy marketplace that has ten
pentacles near some merchants. Prosperity; a very large exchange
of money; riches; business transactions; high material attainment.

WANDS

Ace of Wands   Visualize a beautiful budding wand. Beginning of a
creation; enterprise; a new life.

Two of Wands   Visualize a young male who holds two wands in
one hand and the world in the other. The attainment of goals; a
business venture; courage in plans; two heads are better than one.

Three of Wands   Visualize a male who stands at the edge of a cliff
overseeing the ocean, with three wands to his side. The seeds of
your work will now flourish, unfolding success; enterprise;
negotiations; prosperity.

Four of Wands   Visualize four wands standing upright, decorated
with garlands. In the background are ceremonial grounds. A
wedding ceremony; a social gathering in celebration; gatherings.

Five of Wands   Visualize five young males at war with each other,
using wands as their weapons. Conflicts; battles with other
people; struggles; obstacles.

Six of Wands   Visualize an adorned soldier parading on his horse
through town. He is holding one wand and the other five

wands are around him. Conquest; victory; advancement; recognition; a win.

Seven of Wands   Visualize a young male holding off six battling wands with his one wand. Holding your own against others; trying to overcome obstacles; difficult task but the willingness to fight; a possible loss.

Eight of Wands   Visualize eight flowering wands soaring through the sky. Arrows of love; messages coming; phone calls; journey by air.

Nine of Wands   Visualize an exhausted soldier who is wounded and rests against nine wands. You have fought adequately in previous battles, but there is still one more confrontation to endure.

Ten of Wands   Visualize a man who carries the oppressive load of ten wands. Completion is very soon; a problem to be resolved shortly; the ending of strife toward a long goal.

Pendulum

A pendulum is a weighted device supported by a string or chain, which is able to swing freely. The best pendulums are purchased from occult stores. They are usually made of a metallic material and come in various sizes, shapes, and colors. Some pendulums are hollow inside so you can place specific ingredients inside of them. The ingredient inside will respond to the same ingredient outside of the pendulum. This is commonly used when searching for gold, silver, water, and so forth. Most pendulums are solid. If a pendulum is unavailable, I strongly suggest using a necklace or some sort of pointed metal device and suspending it from a chain.

A pendulum can answer "yes" or "no" questions and also spell out letters. On the "yes" or "no" questions, hold the chain with your dominant hand over the top of the palm of the receiving hand. Ask your Guides to set your pendulum for "yes" and set your pendulum for "no." Nine times out of ten, the "yes" is set in a clockwise motion. The "no" is usually set in a counterclockwise motion. When your pendulum is set, it is ready for divining. Set your pendulum every day before you use it.

When divining for letters or numbers, write on a piece of paper or cloth the same layout as the Ouija board. Letters "A" through "M" on the top, letters "N" through "Z" on the second row. Numbers "0" through "9" on the bottom. Set the pendulum to true or false. The rotation will either be clockwise or counterclockwise.

Under no circumstances should a person divine anything if she is sick, taking strong medications, or has been drinking alcohol. These are absolute law breakers of the Universe. You will not be able to receive any positive answers or any correct answers if you try to divine while under these influences. Even if you have a mild cold, do not do any divining until you are well.

"Yes" or "No"

The following methods will allow you to divine "yes" or "no" questions:

Coin Toss

Use a very special and heavy-weighted coin. Use this coin simply for divining and nothing else. Say this incantation:

> Coin of Toss
> Reveal and Show.
> The Head is Yes,
> The Tail is No.

Flip the coin high in the air and let it fall where it may. The head side is the answer "yes." The tail side is the answer "no."

Water Stones

Obtain ten nearly identical stones that are about one-and-a-half inches in size. They have to be the same color and close to the same size. Inscribe five of them (using waterproof paint or some other method) with the word "yes" and five with the word "no." Place them in a clear, flat-bottomed bowl. In the same bowl, put fresh spring water with three pinches of salt. Put enough water in it so that the stones are definitely submerged. The stones need to be placed with the writing side down so you cannot read them. Say this incantation:

> *Waters clear upon my gaze,*
> *Reveal my answer without haze.*
> *I divine this question that I may see,*
> *If "yes" or "no," So Mote It Be."*

Ask your question out loud. Draw only one stone. The answer is then revealed.

The Wand Spin

Obtain a piece of white silk about twelve inches by twelve inches. Write the four directions on the silk in black ink. Place your wand in the center of the silk. Ask your question. Say this incantation:

> *As I spin this wand of mine,*
> *Reveal the truth of the Divine.*
> *If the crystal points to the North,*
> *The answer is, "Yes, do go forth."*
> *If the crystal points to the South,*
> *The answer is, "No, there is doubt."*
> *If the crystal points to the East,*
> *The answer is, "Yes, do proceed."*
> *If the crystal points to the West,*
> *The answer is, "No, there is no guess."*
> *If the wand stops in between*
> *The four directions upon the sheen,*
> *Then spin again up to three,*
> *Ask the Guides for clarity.*
> *If after three the answer not told,*
> *The truth reveals not silver or gold.*
> *Your answer has gone two different ways,*
> *It is not black or white, but shades of gray.*

Ask your question, then spin the wand. The crystal at the end of your wand is your pointer. If it points to the North or East, the answer is "yes." If it points to the South or West, the answer is "no." If you spin and it goes in between the directions, then spin again. If you spin three consecutive times and the results are still in between, then your answer is totally mixed with positive and negative energy. Your answer is not "maybe," but rather a combination of yes and no.

Divining Buttons

This is a divining that should be done spontaneously. If you are considering a very serious question, but cannot seem to come up with the answer alone, do this little rhyme:

> *Ask your question, then close your eyes.*
> *The person before you will tell no lies.*
> *The very first person whom you will see,*
> *Knows the answer, but does not speak.*
> *Count the buttons upon his wear,*
> *Your answer will come, but do not stare.*
> *If the buttons are even and not one less,*
> *Your answer is definitely one of "yes."*
> *If the buttons are odd and no more show,*
> *Your answer is definitely one of "no."*
> *If a button is missing, then you have guessed,*
> *Your life will be happy and all is blessed.*

Count the buttons on the first person you see after you have asked your question. If the number of buttons are an even number, the answer to your question is "yes." If the number of buttons are an odd number, the answer to your question is "no." If you happen to notice that a button is missing from the person's garment, still count how many buttons and the answer lies in the even or odd number, but the missing button shows you that no matter what happens, you will be very happy and very blessed.

Skipping Rocks

This divining is of the same principle of even and odd numbers. Ask your question out loud, then skip a rock across a smooth body of water. If it skips an even number of times, your answer is "yes." If it skips an odd number of times, your answer is "no."

Divining Dice

Ask your question out loud. Take two dice and toss them. The total number will reveal the answer to your questions:

> *Throw and toss a number two, the answer is yes, it is true.*
> *Throw and toss a number three, the answer is yes, it does agree.*
> *Throw and toss a number four, the answer is no, there is no more.*
> *Throw and toss a number five, the answer is no, this is denied.*
> *Throw and toss a number six, the answer is yes, there is no mix.*
> *Throw and toss a number seven, the answer is yes, just like heaven.*
> *Throw and toss a number eight, the answer is no, it is the fate.*
> *Throw and toss a number nine, the answer is no, it is not fine.*
> *Throw and toss a number ten, the answer is yes, but ask again.*
> *Throw and toss a number eleven, the answer is yes, just like seven.*
> *Throw and toss a number twelve, the answer is no, pity yourself.*

Divining Cards

Ask your question out loud. Have a regular deck of playing cards to divine your answer. Cut the cards into two stacks. The stack on the right side of the diviner tells the influence. The stack on the left side of the diviner tells the answer. Turn over the top card of each two stacks. The following rhyme will tell you your answer.

> *An ace on the right is a delight. An ace on the left is a yes.*
> *A deuce on the right is a rare sight. A deuce on the left is a no.*
> *A three on the right is a bit of a fright. A three on the left is yes.*

A four on the right is very tight. A four on the left is a no.
A five on the right takes a great might. A five on the left is a yes.
A six on the right is very light. A six on the left is no.
A seven on the right takes all night. A seven on the left is a yes.
An eight on the right takes a bite. An eight on the left is a no.
A nine on the right is a longer fight. A nine on the left is a yes.
A ten on the right is the color white. A ten on the left is a no.
A Jack on the right is the right height. A Jack on the left is a yes.
A Queen on the right talks all night. A Queen on the left is a no.
A King on the right relies on the knight. A King on the left is a
yes.

Book Divining

You need either a dictionary or a Bible. Ask your question out loud. Ask your Guides to give you the right answer. With your eyes closed, open to a specific page and place your finger on the area that you feel is correct. Read the verse or the word that you have chosen and that will be your answer.

Divining Bag

In a black velvet bag place seven white marbles and seven black marbles. Say your question out loud. Draw three marbles. The following rhyme will explain the rest.

Bag of mystery—mystery divine!
Reveal yes or no with the magical sign.
One white marble is a yes.
Two white marbles there is no guess.
Three white marbles is a positive sign.
Bag of mystery—mystery divine!
Reveal yes or no with the magickal sign.
One black marble is a no.
Two black marbles say it isn't so.
Three black marbles is a negative sign.

With three marbles drawn, there is a mix,
I must know more, so now I draw six.
If equal be three black and three white,
My mind is closed, my heart is not right.
Replace them all for another draw,
The first one out will tell it all.

The white marbles signify a "yes." The black marbles signify a "no." If six are drawn and three are black and three are white, then the diviner is too close to the situation to see clearly. Replace all marbles and then draw only one. The white or black will tell if it is a "yes" or "no."

Dream Interpretation

The mystery of dreams may elude us forever. Why do dreams even occur? No one really knows for sure. One undeniable fact is that some dreams are absolute prophecy of future events and other dreams are just dreams. Interpreting dreams has been an age-old method of divining. There were dream interpreters before the inspiration of the Bible. If you are trying to divine while you sleep, one method is to simply ask your Guides to reveal the answer to you in your dreams.

Astral projection can occur during the dream state. It has been known that even time warps exist during astral projection in the dream state. There is a significant difference between regular dreams and the experience of astral projection in the dream state. During astral projection, you experience more of a physical sensation.

The following is a brief list of interpretations of dreams:

If you dream	Possible interpretation
Accident	Problems in a relationship
Actor/Actress	The coming of prosperity and fame
Aging	Sickness is close
Airplane	Courage will lead to great success

If you dream	Possible interpretation
Anchor	Something is holding you back or stopping you
Angels	Peace, happiness, or the actual presence of Angels
Anger	Love that has been denied
Apples	Longevity and good health
Ashes	Great misfortune surrounds something
Baby	Joy and happiness
Balding	Sickness is close
Ball	Money is coming unexpectedly
Bat	Danger is approaching
Bathing	Long life is ahead
Beach	Loneliness and solitude
Bed	Changes in marital status
Bells	Good news is approaching
Blood	Loss and disappointment
Boat	Prosperity is ahead
Books	Knowledge and wisdom
Bottle	Secrets are near
Brews	Expect a visitor
Bride	Contracts are pending
Bridge	An overwhelming fear of the future
Cake	Joy, love, and marriage
Candle	A letter will arrive soon
Cats	Unpredictable behavior
Children	Success, abundance, and wealth
Clock	A hasty marriage
Clothes	Fear of showing the true self
Cooking	A party or gathering of friends
Crown	Rise above any situation
Dance	To receive a great honor
Darkness	Sudden change in present conditions
Death	Life is continuing

If you dream	Possible interpretation
Divorce	Fidelity is in question
Doctor	Good health
Dog	Good friends
Dragon	Change of residence
Drowning	Difficulties lie ahead
Earthquake	Loss or quarrel
Engagement	Promises to come
Feather	Omen of possible run of bad luck
Fire	Beware of false friends
Fountain	Laughter
Glass	Prophecy can be seen
Gold	Look for fortune in other areas
Home	Good health and prosperity
Horse	Delay or suspension in time
Ice	Failure in business or love
Journey	Change in circumstances
King	Success is near
Kiss	Beware of false friends
Knife	Ruin and misfortune
Ladder	Movement in a forward position of success
Laughing	Good health
Lightning	Advancement
Lion	Courage and strength are needed
Marriage	Uncertain of self-worth
Mice	Beware of social contacts
Mirror	Disappointment
Money	Look for fortune in other areas
Mountain	Increase of love and money
Music	Pleasures and sensuality
Needle	Divining is necessary
Neighbor	Gossip
Nun	Loneliness and solitude
Ocean	Reconciliation

If you dream	Possible interpretation
Old	Good fortune is yet to come
Owl	Do not tell secrets
Paint	Upheaval in the home
Pins	Quarrels
Policeman	Disputes will be settled soon
Postman	News from afar
Queen	Success is near
Rain	A present or gift is coming
Rat	Triumph over enemies
Raven	Death
Ring	Wedding or marriage
River	Envy and jealousy
Rock	The present situation cannot be changed
Rose	Success
Running	A journey is in the future
Salt	Good fortune and wisdom
Ship	Riches
Singing	Double imagery
Snow	Prosperity
Sun	Success, wealth, and love
Swim	Troubles are ahead
Talking	Too many worries
Teeth	Sickness and pressures
Thief	Loss in every aspect
Tunnel	Trouble will pass soon
Unicorn	Escape
Unknown Person	Return of a loved one
Veil	Look behind the scenes
Violets	Success and power
Vulture	Misfortune
Walking	Time needed for contemplation
Watch	Journey is ahead
Water	Reconciliation

If you dream	Possible interpretation
Waves	Prepare to fight
Well	Profit
Witch	Discovery of many secrets
Wolf	Danger in solitude
Worms	Sickness
X-Rays	Beware of Peeping Toms
Youth	Time to emphasize beauty
Zebra	Disagreement with friends

Scrying

To read a crystal ball or a magickal mirror is a technique called scrying. Scrying has been in existence for thousands of years. The first known acts of scrying were done by using reflections on a lake. To scry means to have the ability of seeing psychic visions. The visions can represent past, present, or future events, as well as answers to many questions.

When purchasing a crystal ball, look for those that have great clarity and very few bubbles. When purchasing a magickal mirror, look for mirrors that are especially light in reflection. The crystal ball should always be placed in some sort of stand so that it does not roll or move. The magickal mirror should be placed flat. Surround both the crystal ball and magickal mirror with candles. Many crystal balls and mirrors are anointed with special blends of olive oil and herbs before using.

Align the chakras and call upon your Guides prior to scrying. When reading either the crystal ball or mirror, rely on your third eye for seeing. Sometimes the mind can pick things up as totally visual, but it is really the third eye that *sees*.

The symbols that are usually seen are clouds, colors, images, and movements. When seeing clouds, note the color and whether there is any movement. The following are clues to help interpret the reading.

An image that has color denotes the following:

White	purity and wholeness
Blue	peace and tranquillity
Yellow	health and happiness
Orange	attraction
Red	anger, accident, or passion
Pink	love, friendship, or romance
Green	money of any kind
Purple	psychic power
Black	bad omen

Any movements denote:

Moving North	a yes
Moving South	a no
Moving East	positive favor
Moving West	people and places make differences

The various images can be related to the same interpretations as the dream divining (see Dream Interpretations).

Both the crystal ball and the magickal mirror are powered by the Moon and governed by the Goddess. Both should be consecrated and magnetized with your energy and the Moon's energy. There should not be any sunlight on either of these oracles. When the crystal ball and magickal mirror are not in use, cover them with a dark cloth that is soft and has no rough or scratchy fibers.

According to the Qabala tradition, there should be seven magickal mirrors:

Use on Sunday	a gold mirror
Use on Monday	a silver mirror
Use on Tuesday	an iron mirror
Use on Wednesday	a mercury mirror

Use on Thursday   a tin mirror
Use on Friday   a copper mirror
Use on Saturday   a lead mirror

These mirrors correspond to the planetary influence.

Divining by Runes

Runes are letters from an alphabet with magickal properties. The literal word *rune* means "mystery" or "secret." Runes are symbols etched on individual stones. There are twenty-five stones in all. They are kept in a bag until they are used. To use runes, simply draw them out and read them. There are numerous spreads, but the simplest and most explicit is the three-draw method. Runes are drawn blindly by the diviner.

First, meditate on your question. Then draw the first rune and place it directly in front of yourself. Draw the second rune and place it to the left. Draw the third rune and place it to the right of center. Now you have three runes directly before you; read them right to left. The first position shows the question as to where it is right now. The second position shows the problems or obstacles presented in the question. The third position reveals the outcome and advice to the question. Unlike "yes" or "no" divining, the runes are to be considered self-transformation and they give insight about how to deal with the question.

Runes are highly spiritual and are governed by the God. It is advised to never ask a repeat question to the runes. One question will have one answer. It should be accepted and regarded as Divine. Out of the twenty-five runes, there are fifteen that are read upright or reverse.

Rune symbols date back to the prehistoric Neolithic and Bronze Ages, dating 8000 B.C. to 2000 B.C. They were drawn or carved into the walls of caves. By the year 100 A.D., runes were widespread over five different continents. The meanings are still very similar to the runes we know today. People even marked their graves with rune symbols to ward off grave robbers. By the fourteenth century, runes were banned by the Church. Like all classic pieces of magick, the runes somehow survived.

The following is a brief description of how to read the runes:

 The Self Willingness to change is effective now. Remain receptive. To thine own self be true. Do the task for the task's sake. Live an ordinary life in an unordinary way.

 The Self in Reverse Change patterns or past habits. If you feel blocked, look within yourself. Recognize the source of what is coming from yourself.

 Partnership A union or merger of two is near. It may range from love to union with the higher self. Retain your identity in this union.

 Signals Receiving messages, signals, gifts, and so forth. You must first give to yourself before you can give to others. Pay attention to all meetings, visits, or chance encounters.

 Signals in Reverse Concern is lack of communication, lack of clarity or awareness. There is futility in wasted motion. What is happening is timely. Consider the uses of adversity.

 Retreat You may take a radical departure from old ways. Do not be too mechanical or unaware. See clearly.

 Strength Prepare for opportunities disguised as loss. There may be a death within yourself. Termination and new beginnings are activated. To grow involves going into a place of darkness.

 Strength in Reverse It may seem that your own strength is working against you. The numbed senses, missed opportunities, disappointments, or minor failures are felt too hard.

Initiation   Secret and hidden games are likely. Take a broader vision and the freedom to find that wholeness is a profound secret.

 Initiation in Reverse   Do not expect too much. Organize your own energy and try not to be scattered. Concentrate on your own life. Be patient and be constant.

 Constraint   Recognize limitations that you directly cause yourself. Restore balance and confidence. Do not take the world so seriously.

 Constraint in Reverse There is a great teacher disguised as pain. The suffering means you are going through a dark side of life's passage.

 Fertility   Intuition is strong. Completion of a beginning process. Deliverance. A new life or new path is near. Prioritize for completion.

 Defense   There is blockage in your path. This is a time of patience and fortitude. Foresight is needed. Set things in order and tend to business.

 Protection   Control is necessary. Do not give in to your own weakness or self-pity. New opportunities are at hand. Progress is your protection. Do not avoid, hide, or deny this process. Face it head on.

 Protection in Reverse   Be considerate of your health. Look carefully at all associations, especially if people are using you. Take only your own responsibilities. Use temperance and courtesy.

 Possessions   Fulfillment and ambitions are the rewards. Love is satisfied. Enjoy good fortune and do not behave recklessly. Do not collapse into success.

 Possessions in Reverse   Frustration is overtaking you. Your efforts fall short and what you have gained is slowly dwindling away. Understand and obtain only what you truly need to survive.

Joy   This is now the coming of a full circle. New energy and clarity are nearing. The bad shift is over and you have already paid your dues.

Joy in Reverse   Things are slow in coming to fruition. Crisis and difficulties are near. Everything you do is a test. Refocus. Stop anxiety and doubt.

Harvest   Beneficial outcome to any endeavor to which you are committed. There are no quick results. Perseverance and patience are encouraged.

The Opening   Renewed clarity and lightness. This is a time for seriousness and concentration. You are at the beginning of an important journey.

The Opening in Reverse   Expect darkness and void. You may lose an opportunity because you're not able to see what is ahead. The end of one way of life and change will promote growth.

Warrior   The battle is within you. Stay out of your own way. Molding your character is an issue here. Romance is timely. Prioritize.

Warrior in Reverse   Hasty actions scatter your energy. Do not behave recklessly. Look within yourself. Do the task for the task's sake.

Growth   Modesty and patience are called for here. Remove resistance and obstacles and accomplish the work. A new beginning is in process.

Growth in Reverse   Events or obstacles of the person can detain growth. Try again with correct preparation and forge ahead.

Movement   Gradual development and steady progress are in motion.

Movement in Reverse   Find the blockage in your life and remove the problem. A new opportunity is at hand.

Flow   Unconscious power. A time to reorganize. This relates to oneself, dealing with intuition, emotion, relationships, and business.

Flow in Reverse   Failure to believe your own intuition. Do not overreact because of your lack of faith. Draw upon wisdom to correct the problem.

Disruption   A need to break free. Outside forces are at work here. Expect a disruption in plans. You are not without power.

Journey   Do not force anything to happen. Find your inner worth. Use meditation and prayer. Self-change and self-healing will overcome obstacles. The union is within yourself.

Journey in Reverse   Interruptions in your relationships. Efforts and wisdom are required. Detours, obstacles, and blockages can actually bring new opportunities.

Gateway   Find the worth inside and outside of yourself. This is not a good time to make decisions. You have difficulty in seeing what lies within you.

Gateway in Reverse   Do not suffer over suffering. Do not fall into self-pity. Do not create more problems by hasty decisions. There is growth and progress, but there are delays as well.

Breakthrough   Major shift. A 180-degree turn. Outcome is assured but not predictable. A lot of hard work is involved. Transform your life.

Standstill   Stalemate. Bound by blockage. Drained energy. Positive accomplishment is unlikely. Be patient and let go of whatever is holding you.

Wholeness   Self-realization. Individual power will surge. This is a force of what you are to become. Do not force anything.

The Unknowable   The beginning and the end of your destiny. Fate. This is total potential. Many fears, dreams, and opportunities are here. Karma.

9

SABBATS
AND ESBATS

Light the fire beneath the pot,
Thirteen moons in the lot.
Four days high, four days not,
Solstice and the equinox.
Gather 'round for the feast,
North, South, West, and East.
Bless the children and the beasts,
Gather Crones, Witches, and Priests.
Cleanse the tools and the day,
Sing and dance, laugh and play.
Honor the moon to which we pray,
Celebrate the Wiccan way.

BELLADONNA

The Wiccans have eight high holidays known as Sabbats. Four of the eight are major Sabbats known as Fire Festivals. The other four are minor Sabbats that correspond to the seasons.

There are twelve to thirteen full moons in a year. The gathering under a full moon to do ritual work is called an Esbat. The word *Esbat* literally means "to frolic under the moon." Witches are very serious about ritual work but after the work is done, Witches are highly festive. Esbats are always enjoyable.

The four minor Sabbats are always on the day the seasons change, such as the summer and winter solstices, and the vernal and autumnal equinoxes. *Solstice* means the days with the sun's longest and shortest duration. The sun's longest day is about June 22 and the sun's shortest day is about December 22. *Equinox* means the days when daylight and night are roughly equal in time, which are about March 22 and about September 22.

The coven will vote which Sabbats and which Esbats they will gather on. The Sabbats should be recognized even if the coven does not convene.

Performing rituals on the Full Moon with or without the coven is also important. I have found that doing rituals on the night of the Full Moon either by myself or with the coven makes the entire month go better. In total, there are twenty to twenty-one specific days each year that should be honored by the practicing Witch. There are other important days on which special magick can be performed rather than on Sabbats and Esbats.

The Eight Sabbats

March 22: Spring Equinox

OSTARA

Minor Sabbat. Time to plant seeds, reconcile differences, focus on health issues, rebirth, change, life begins, the Goddess awakens and spreads fertility. Time of dedication and purpose.

Ritual Suggestion: Choose an indoor plant you wish to grow from either a seed or small rooting. Choose the plant that best represents what you desire to start for the year. Example: Peppermint for prosperity or an aloe vera for healing, and so forth. Write an incantation for your own self-growth. Choose the appropriate candle, oil, and incense. Burn the incantation and bury the ashes in the soil of your new plant. As the plant grows, so will your wish.

May 1: Beltane

MAY DAY

Major Sabbat. Time to rejoice in the rebirth of the world; the God has reached his manhood. Time for beauty, wealth, a fertility feast, the mystic union of the God and the Goddess. The festive colors of red and white should dominate; make flower baskets, maypoles, colored eggs, and passionate love.

Ritual Suggestions: (1) Wash your face in the early morning dew (before 6:00 A.M.) to make your skin beautiful. (2) Erect a maypole with the colors of red and white ribbon striping the main pole. (3) Create a flower basket with bright-colored flowers. Inside of the basket, place special offerings that are fit for a God and place it secretly on the porch of your beloved. (4) Color hard-boiled eggs and serve them at your Beltane Feast. (5) Crack an egg in a glass of water. Light a candle near the yoke and scry the future. (6) Create a special dance, including leaping over fire for good luck. (7) Skim some water from a wealthy person's well. Pour half of what you skimmed back and carry the rest home. You are sharing their fortune. All wells are magickal.

June 22: Summer Solstice

LITHA

Minor Sabbat. The longest day of the year. This is also known as midsummer's day. Time to collect magickal herbs for the winter. Time of peak power. The colors that should dominate this festival are red and yellow. Ivy is bountiful. Time to find the field Faeries. Talk to the elves and ask them to do your bidding. Festival of strength and clear sight.

Ritual Suggestions: (1) Walk naked through a garden at night to become fertile. (2) Bathe in a stream at midnight so the Faeries will approach you. (3) When harvesting magickal herbs, cut away only two-thirds of the plants and leave the other one-third to assure their growth. On this night it is time to harvest the mandrake. Do not let the mandrake scream when being pulled or you will be cursed. (4) Take a wand made of hazel wood to divine hidden treasures. (5) Create a decorative wreath with fallen feathers.

August 1: Lammas

LUGHNASSADH

Major Sabbat. The God is starting to weaken. The Goddess feels the stirring of the unborn child. No vines should be cut. No washing should be done on this day. This is the first harvest of fruits and grains. The days start to shorten. This is a festival for the Faeries. A time of completion. Harvest the remaining magickal herbs. Be thankful for the bounty. Prepare for autumn.

Ritual Suggestions: (1) Prepare a feast with bread as the main course. The bread represents the God. Decorate your altar with the bounty of the first harvest—fruits and vegetables. (2) Change table-cloths, curtains, and any material that decorates the home. (3) Complete all started projects. (4) Brooms should be cleaned and ready.

September 22: Autumn Equinox

MABON

Minor Sabbat. The veil between worlds grows thin. Time for personal balance. The God is preparing to die. The Goddess is in complete bounty. Time of the second harvest. Rest. Fill the emotional and mental well within. Time to honor the rivers and streams. Corn is the major harvest. All remaining herbs or plants should be harvested now. The decorative colors of the festival should be orange, red, gold, and brown. Prepare the cornucopia. Time for endings. Time to purify. The Goddess prepares for the God to die.

Ritual Suggestions: (1) Excellent time for poppets and dolls made from corn. (2) Collect the fallen leaves to make a wreath. (3) Bind all the negative energy and put an end to problems. (4) Prepare potions dealing with vinegar. (5) Toast the God with cider and corn cakes. (6) Cast spells dealing with debt removal or the ending of communications and relationships.

October 31: Samhain Eve

ALL HALLOW'S EVE

Major Sabbat. The God has died. The final harvest. The veil between worlds is now at its weakest. The spirits in the other world can now pass into this world, but only for twenty-four hours. Spirits of all kinds pass. The average person should wear a disguise to confuse the entities. Witches should dress as Witches so they can be identified by the entities. The Witches will welcome the *wanted* spirits to feast with the coven and also help send back the *unwanted* spirits. Time to honor the dead. Time to rest. The festival should be decorated in the colors of orange and black. The feast should include all of the bounty of the last harvest.

Ritual Suggestions: (1) Offer gourds and cornucopia to the altar. Toast all of the invited spirits that have passed over to feast with you. Prepare a completed plate for the dead. (2) Perform a ritual séance to open the veil. (3) Scatter pumpkin seeds to promote romance.

(4) Offer a special ritual for all of the persecuted Witches of the past. (5) Have the coven make a special pillow and quilt for the Goddess to lay Her head on and rest. (6) Pledge to all of the Quarters and magickal elements that have helped you in your time of need.

December 22: Winter Solstice

YULE

Minor Sabbat. The rebirth of the God. The pledge of the returning sun. The shortest day of the year. Fire festival includes the Yule log. The colors of this festival are red and green. The beginning of the death of winter. Time for rest to be nearing the end. Time of enlightenment. Awakenment of life. Another star is added to the sky. Time to increase intelligence.

Ritual Suggestions: (1) Burning the Yule log symbolizes peace and protection in the home. Ashes from the Yule log are placed at the base of fruit trees to assure fruitfulness. Keep a small piece of the Yule log in the home to promote peace throughout the year. (2) Bayberry is used in rituals to promote wealth and prosperity. (3) Wreaths of holly and ivy are made for protection. (4) Kiss under the mistletoe for luck and love. (5) Gifts of corn and other grains placed around trees for the wildlife promotes love and bounty within the home. (6) Giving gifts promotes harmony of the heart.

February 1: Candlemas

IMBOLC

Major Sabbat. Celebration involving the banishing of winter. Fire festival dedicated to burning out the old and bringing in the new. The feast of candles. The days are getting longer. The Boy-God is growing and learning. Purification. A time for changes. This is a festival of fertility. The Goddess is alive with anticipation. Time to burn out the darkness in our lives with the power of the sun. Time to sprout. Time to take care of the animals. Time to prepare for underground seeds. The dominant colors are lavender and white.

Ritual Suggestions: (1) Light candles of all colors. Do not extinguish any candles. Let the candles burn themselves out to symbolize the power of the sun. (2) Fertility rituals begin. (3) Light all candles after sunset to honor the God. (4) Rituals of purification in honor of the Goddess. (5) Sweep out all negative and stagnant energy. (6) Rituals involving wine and cakes. (7) Rituals involving the burning of shrouds.

Esbats

January: The Wolf Moon

Rituals for independence, good fortune, and for change of luck in general. Rituals for protection in and around the home, and rituals for healing the Earth. Rituals that pertain to the underprivileged: the hungry, the homeless, the sick, the needy, and so forth. Rituals for divining future partners, happiness in general, and rituals honoring the Goddess.

February: The Storm Moon

Rituals for protection against poverty. Rituals for family harmony, strengthening existing relationships, and for better communication in general. Rituals for rededication of purpose and strengthening mind and memory. Body and spirit cleansing. Rituals for travelers and animals. Rituals for legal assistance when needed and protection from those who fight against you. Rituals for purity of heart. Rituals to detour harmful gossip. Rituals for attraction in the love areas.

March: The Chaste Moon

Rituals for freedom and new beginnings. Rituals for banishing sickness, despair, and bad luck. Rituals for fertility, abundance, and growth. Rituals for children, flowers, and the life force. Rituals for good judgment and for positive actions. Rituals for mothers in general. Rituals that honor the Moon and psychic energies. Rituals to promote dream divining and clairvoyance. Rituals honoring the mind and body.

April: The Seed Moon

Rituals for planting in general. Rituals for good crop growth and for good weather magick. Rituals for flowers and for things of beauty. Rituals for all kinds of travel. Rituals to banish fear and sadness. Rituals for new beginnings. Rituals for proper balance, good decisions, and for truth. Rituals to dispel old and new anger, to dispel problems of all kinds, and to release issues that involve hate. Rituals for progress and movement toward goals.

May: The Lover's Moon

Rituals for the Goddess, mothers in general, and for female energies. Rituals for cleansing the mind, body, and spirit. Rituals for the home and family. Rituals for love in new and existing relationships. Rituals for fertility. Rituals for prosperity, bounty, and abundance. Rituals to honor the Crones of past, present, and future. Rituals for beauty, the body, and for perfection. Rituals to celebrate the conception of the God into the Goddess.

June: The Honey Moon

Rituals for marriages and life partners. Rituals for love. Rituals for unions and reunions. Rituals for wisdom, physical strength, and endurance. Rituals for the Earth to be in bounty. Celebration of Earth products. Rituals for maidens to search for inner truth and self-respect. Rituals for young males to find physical and mental strength. Rituals for conception. Rituals that incorporate upcoming initiations. Celebrations that involve the bounty of the Earth.

July: The Festive Moon

Rituals for peace, protection, and harmony. Rituals to celebrate marriages and for life partners. Rituals for freedom and choices. Rituals for karmic completion. Rituals for enlightenment and intuition. Rituals to celebrate the bounty of crops and the bounty of life. Rituals to celebrate the fertility of animals. Rituals to promote world peace. Rituals for harvesting magickal herbs. Rituals for thankfulness to the Goddess and God for all individual blessings.

August: The Poet's Moon

Rituals for writing, creating, and performing old and new spells. Rituals for the first harvest. Rituals for Witches to celebrate the freedom of choice regarding their religion. Rituals for removing obstacles and any obstruction of goals. Rituals for perfumes, oils, and incenses. Rituals involving asking Faeries, gnomes, and elves to do one's bidding for Earth's protection. Rituals involving the Quadrants and their elements. Rituals to promote playtimes, fantasies, and daydreams.

September: The Fire Moon

Rituals honoring the second harvest. Rituals for change. Rituals for banishing all that is negative. This is a time for bonfires. Rituals dealing with thankfulness for bounty, dancing, and gardening. Rituals dealing with oracles, divining, and rededication of the Wiccan tools. Rituals to banish useless and negative influences, including addictions. Rituals to preserve life and youth. Rituals to uncover secrets and discover treasures.

October: The Harvest Moon

Rituals honoring the third and final harvest. Rituals for protection and safety during travels. Rituals involving the celebration of life and the celebration of the eternal life that exists on the other side. Rituals for clocks, brooms, and graveyards. Rituals honoring the eternal nests and all employment areas. Rituals for the release of grieving and suffering. Rituals dealing with healings and clearings.

Rituals involving the light and the dark of the sun. The ritual that pays tribute to the death of the God.

November: The Hunter's Moon

Rituals honoring the Angels who do the bidding and the Angels who do the guiding. Rituals that involve peace and comfort. Rituals that involve the blessing of the kitchen and the hearth. Rituals dealing with sunsets, brothers and sisters, mourning, cleanliness, and purification. Rituals involving honor, rest, the cauldron, and protection of the woodlands. Rituals honoring animals and weavings. Time to quilt and to repair or refurbish altars. Time to purify wells. Rituals involving peace among family and friends.

December: The Laughing Moon

Rituals honoring the birth of the God child. Rituals involving success, prosperity, and bounty. Rituals dealing with births, beginnings, babies, mothers, and Crones. Rituals involving reincarnation and life. Rituals to banish the sleeping and the stillness. Rituals involving laughing, happiness, and harmony. Rituals honoring parents and the life cycle of nature. Rituals dealing with winter Faeries. Rituals involving wishes and hopes. Rituals involving gifts and generosity. Rituals to gently awaken the sleeping souls.

The Thirteenth Moon: The Blue Moon

Rituals involving special blessings. Rituals to inspire and rededicate one's life purpose. A time to have completeness. Rituals involving love, prosperity, and good health. Rituals involving fantasies that need to be realities. Rituals designed to make new and higher goals. Rituals involving brooms and purification of magickal tools and cupboards. Rituals involving the lives of others so that they may see their dreams come true. Ceremonies that require dressing up in disguise. High-intensity psychic energies.

Invitations and Symbols

Wiccan invitations are always unique. Some covens send out invitations for each gathering while other covens send them out only for special gatherings, such as Wiccanings, High Priestesshood, Croning, Handfasting, and Birth Rites. All invitations are done in Wiccan symbols. The front of the invitation describes the event. The inside of the invitation provides the details. The purpose of the invitation is to inform and invite, the twist of the invitation is that no one else can decipher the message except for a Witch.

SYMBOLS

Covenstead

A.M.

P.M.

Esbat

Sabbat

Wiccaning

High Priestess

Croning

Handfast

Birth Rite

Bring food

Bring drink

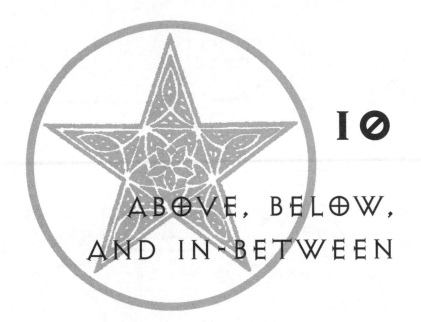

10

ABOVE, BELOW, AND IN-BETWEEN

The sitters of the circle gather,
The spirit board begins to rock.
Messages from another world,
Speak before they knock.
The Angels come to protect them,
Shrouded within the sphere.
Demons below are clawing,
And planting seeds of fear.
The ghosts are anxiously waiting,
For the Medium's call.
A frozen breath upon a neck,
Invites not one, but all.
The gates of heaven are open,
The Angels are often seen.
The doors of hell are broken,
Unleashing in between.

BELLADONNA

Angels

The definition of an Angel is an immortal being who exists in the Spirit World but serves between two worlds. In Greek *Angel* means "messenger." Their main purpose is to give messages to us. There are black angels living between earth and hell, as well. I prefer to acknowledge them as Dark Forces instead of Angels. The word *Angel* just feels very divine and pure to me. As stated in chapter 1, not all Witches believe there is a heaven or hell. I believe in both and that there is a ruler in hell, known as Satan. The Dark Forces are mere followers of evil.

The questions come to us sooner or later: "How does one become an Angel? And, if our soul reincarnates, then how do you explain Angels?" I believe every soul has a destination. It can rest and learn in either Heaven or hell, or even become a ghost on an earthly plane, but all souls have a destination. I believe some souls are older than others. The older, the wiser, and the more pure of heart the soul is, the more likely the candidate is to become an Angel. I also believe the Goddess and God can select which souls They want to become Angels. Earning the right to become an Angel and the timing of this is totally up to the individual.

Angels communicate telepathically. This means sending and receiving messages by way of the mind. The difference between intuition and messages from Angels is the way it is said. In an Angel message there is a certain peace that vibrates with every word. The messages from Angels are always valid. Listen.

There are seven different categories of Angels, just as there are seven levels of Heaven. Some Angels have more range and power than other Angels. Some Angels even have the power to materialize before us. I do not believe anyone knows the exact layout of Heaven or the exact range of power the Angels have. Those people who have had near-death experiences have a special view of Heaven and the passageway to it, whereas the rest of us can only speculate. A near-death experience is when a person has physically died for a short period of time and then somehow has returned to their physical body. These individuals are usually greeted on the other side by Angels and are also escorted back by Angels.

The Seven Types of Angels

1. *Archangels* The highest of all Angels. Their assignment is to serve the Goddess and God. They are the closest to the Deities and their power is enormous.

2. *Quadrant Angels* These are the Angels we call upon in our ritual work. The four Angels—Raphael, Michael, Gabriel, and Uriel—are the department heads. Numerous other Angels are working as Quadrant Angels. Their assignment is to govern and protect the Earth and its inhabitants.

3. *Guardian Angels* Everyone is born with a Guardian Angel. This is the Angel who sharpens our intuitive senses. When we contemplate an idea that may involve hurting someone or something, this Angel tugs at our heart. These Angels have a mid-range of power. Reasoning is one of their top skills. The Guardian Angel can be denounced by an individual, but this would leave that person without an Angel.

4. *Healing Angels* These Angels are the miracle workers who physically, mentally, and emotionally heal people and animals, as instructed by the Goddess and God. Their power is restricted to healing and healing miracles.

5. *Prayer Angels* These Angels are listening to and recording our prayers. Every prayer we speak is recorded and submitted to the Goddess and God for approval, disapproval, or delay.

Sometimes when we think our prayers are being denied, they are just being delayed.

6. *Special Angels*   The Special Angels have an awesome job. They have complete diversity in their work and can achieve almost any miracle. Their main focus is to help individuals complete their karmic cycles.

7. *Escorting Angels*   These are the transporters from this world into the next. Some people refer to the Angel of Death when talking about this kind of Angel. The Angel of Death is supposedly cloaked in black and prepares the family for the exit of a loved one. The appearance of this Angel is to serve as a warning or preparation. The other Escorting Angels are not as ominous-looking, and they very gently remove the soul from the body and transport it to the proper destination.

I was privileged enough to watch a Special Angel at work in the life of one of my clients. I met my client the day after Christmas, 1992. She was very distraught because her husband of sixteen years asked her for a divorce. He was a very busy man, the father of her five children, and a prominent attorney in a large city. He was rarely home, maybe six or seven hours a night, then off again to his busy career. When my client married him, she worked two jobs to put him through law school. The plan was to inflate his career first, and then she could go to school. The five children came along early in the marriage and my client was extremely blessed and satisfied with being a full-time mother. Her career would have to wait until after the children were older. She had absolutely no clue that her husband was unhappy in the marriage. After all, he rarely came home or spent time with the family. How could she know?

When I did the reading for this woman, my heart sank. It was painfully obvious which path this marriage was on. I told her the truth of what I had seen and felt. The marriage had been over for quite some time. There was no hope of putting this marriage back together; the end of the road was here. The woman broke down and cried uncontrollably. I remember praying, asking the Goddess and God to please comfort this woman and to have something special in store for her. I sensed she was an honest, hard-working woman who deserved better. She managed to accept my words even though they were painful. By June their divorce was final. The husband had no real interest in the children but was very unhappy about the child support. He was also unhappy that she was able to smile again and began dating a very nice man. It was just too much for the husband's ego to handle. He soon revealed that he had been having a secret affair and announced his plans to marry the woman, hoping this would be the final blow to his now ex-wife. He put my client through every legal hoop and expense he could think of. She still smiled. By August of the same year, my client had won the lottery and became a millionaire. I do not believe I have ever seen a man so angry in all of my life. He even took her to court in an attempt to get half of her winnings. He lost. Then he took her to court as an unfit mother. He lost. He took her to court to say she should pay him alimony. He lost. He took her to court saying she could not go back to college. He lost. The Special Angel watching out for this woman and her children was having a heyday. I thank the Goddess and God for the smile she wears.

Good Spirits

There are Good Spirits, who can also aid our lives, but they are not Angels. There are also some black spirits who can disrupt our lives, but they are not demons. It is for this reason we acknowledge there are different kinds of ghosts and spirits, and different kinds of encounters we can experience.

The wise Witch summons the Angels and Good Spirits when divining and doing ritual work. The Good Spirits are able to go back and forth between Heaven and earth, and although they have no real power they do have positive energy and effect. They are learning spirits and at some point will reincarnate back to earth when their education is complete. These spirits are learning cosmic perfection or perfect evolution.

Saints

There is a difference between Angels, Good Spirits, and Saints. A Saint is a person who has lived an exceptionally holy life on earth and, when passing over to the other side, has gone on to be of special aid to those of us who pray to them. A Good Spirit is the soul of a genuinely loving person who has passed over to the other side. A Good Spirit has many other lifetimes to reincarnate into but can still help us just the same. Saints and Angels do not reincarnate. They have completed all of their spiritual knowledge and fulfilled all necessary karmic debts. The Good Spirits still have karmic debts that need to be worked out. The Good Spirits have to complete their cosmic cycles of perfection.

It is most effective to communicate with Saints and Angels by way of prayer. Saying the prayer out loud is also more effective than by telepathy. When spell casting, saying the incantation out loud is the same as praying out loud. When trying to communicate with the Good Spirits, prayer does work but there are also other ways.

Ghosts and Apparitions

There have been many theories about time warps. A ghost is a prime example of a time warp. Abraham Lincoln is a ghost at the White House, who sees the building as it was in 1865. There have been hauntings reported where footsteps were heard on a staircase, when there was no staircase . . . the sound of old music playing, when no such music was even in the house. A ghost is stuck in time. A ghost is a disembodied spirit who is usually bound to the Earth. Ghosts are earthbound for different reasons. Some are bound because of sudden trauma at the time of death, an incomplete area of work, love, a lack of spiritual belief, or simply the will to stay behind. Ghosts also are not usually aware they have died. They feel that people are ignoring them.

Many souls of executed people seem to stay earthbound. Sometimes, unfortunately, their anger keeps them around. Energies of anger will cause poltergeist activities. The definition of a poltergeist is a noisy ghost, but there is nothing playful about these types of hauntings. They are usually black spirits. Anger or other negative emotions will propel their energy to manifest. Nothing positive can occur when poltergeists are active. A strange twist to a poltergeist is they can manifest themselves from other people's energies. Anger, fear, and other negative emotions can actually feed them energy, thus causing a reaction or paranormal activity. Teenagers have strong energies that poltergeists can feed from, and children have the next most potent energies. Rarely do poltergeists feed on the energy of adults living in normal realms, but an adult with hate, anger, or depression can certainly promote energy for poltergeists. Poltergeists are not just harmless ghosts; they are negative souls who want to interfere with life. It is important for the Witch to learn how to communicate with these entities and to let them know they are capable of crossing over to the other side.

An apparition is the appearance of a person, animal, or object that is either alive or dead and appears unexpectedly. The words *ghost* and *apparition* are often interchanged, but an apparition does not have to be dead and ghosts are dead. An apparition always wears clothes as does a ghost, but the ghost will wear clothes dating it to the time period when it was alive. An example of an apparition: A mother is busy doing laundry when she looks out of the corner of her eye and sees her son standing in the doorway. She knows for a fact he is away at school. The apparition fades. At that very moment her son falls on the playground at school and breaks his arm. Did the son really appear to the mother at the same time of the accident? Yes. The mother experienced an apparition of her son at the time the accident occurred.

Seven types of apparitions are known to exist:

1. *The Crisis Apparition*   They appear before a catastrophe or a death to serve as a warning. (The Gray Man off the coast of South Carolina appears before a hurricane hits.)

2. *An Apparition of the Recently Deceased*   They appear to loved ones who are grieving. This is to comfort them and let them know they are all right. (The Angel Girl who died in an automobile accident and came back to her mother and grandmother to comfort them.)

3. *The Collective Apparition*   They appear before more than one witness at the same time. (The sightings of the Blessed Virgin.)

4. *Reciprocal Apparition*   When two people see each other at the same time even though they are separated by distance. (Two people writing letters to each other on the same day, at the same time.)

5. *Veridical Apparition*   Supported by undisputed facts. A premonition, message, or appearance to someone who has no way of knowing the facts ahead of time. (A mother tells her son not to go to a friend's house because of a bad feeling she has, and the next day the paper says there was a shooting at the house.)

6. *The Deathbed Apparition*   When a person who is dying is visited by a deceased loved one, a religious figure, an Angel, and so forth, before he or she actually dies. (The old woman who spoke to her deceased mother an hour before she passed. People who experience this are able to leave this world with great peace.)

7. *The Announcing Apparition*   When a deceased person appears to a loved one to announce the birth of a baby. It appears either in total consciousness or in dreams. (The woman in Pennsylvania who saw the apparition of her recently deceased husband telling her she would bring his son into the world in eight-and-a-half months.)

When a Witch is investigating a house with paranormal activity or a person who appears to be possessed, there are a few guidelines to remember. When dealing with ghosts or apparitions, do not assume they are threatening or bad. Investigate *why* the spirit may have stayed behind and what its intentions are. If the ghost is hanging on to a negative emotion, ask it to move on. When dealing with ghosts, plead with them to find the Light or another plane of existence because this plane does not accept them.

A professionally trained person who studies paranormal activity is called a parapsychologist. Whenever there is paranormal activity in a house, a parapsychologist is usually called in to investigate the situation. What would appear to be hauntings are sometimes a case of psychokinesis (PK). Psychokinetics are people who have the ability to move things with their minds. If there is activity in the home and no feeling of ghosts, then keep psychokinesis in mind. Express calmness and consider family counseling to get rid of anger and abrupt emotions. Most of the time the psychokinesis is a subconscious activity, which means the people who are causing the activity have no idea they are actually making things move. The well-trained person who has this ability can make all sorts of things move without touching them. The person who is unaware of this gift is usually the one responsible for paranormal activity in the home. Psychokinesis is spurred by emotions. If a gifted person with high PK gets angry, she can make appliances explode, light bulbs burst, objects move, and so forth. A good Witch should be equally or more skilled than a parapsychologist. Just because a parapsychologist studies the paranormal does not mean that person is intuitive. A good Witch relies upon her intuition. She can sense what is PK activity and what is truly a haunting.

When a Witch is investigating a house with paranormal activity, she should first determine what is making things happen. Where is the *heart* of the activity? She needs to sense where the events are occurring. If there are no cold spots or unusual activities while you are investigating, this does not mean the house is not haunted. Demonic activity does not always manifest in an obvious manner from the start. Ghosts will usually hang around the house and will have a central area. Keep in mind the live inhabitants of the house. Are there any teenagers? Is everyone calm?

When investigating hauntings, make a mental checklist of what you feel, hear, sense, smell, and see. If the ghost is harmless, you may smell roses. If there is a foul smell, it is a demon. If there is no smell, it may be PK activity. Take your time and pay attention. Let your intuition lead you.

A special psychic talent of holding an object and being able to tell who it belongs to is called psychometry. This gift can play an important role in hauntings. The house alone will have its own energy derived from whoever used to live there. A photograph will have the same vibration an object has. Psychometry can aid haunting investigations because it can explain who, what, when, and why.

Parapsychologists use the terms *incarnate* and *discarnate* energies. Incarnate is energy that has a body. Discarnate is energy that has no body.

Spirit Communications

A séance is a gathering of people who wish to communicate with the other side. A Medium is the conductor of the séance. A séance is a very effectual way to communicate to the Good Spirits, but it is also a way to communicate to the not-so-good spirits. An experienced Medium is a truly gifted psychic who knows immediately what kind of spirit is on the other end of the communication. During the 1800s, a Medium was always in demand at socials and tea parties. Today gifted Mediums are few and far between. By the late 1800s, the world had made a mockery of séances and Mediums. Too many Mediums had resorted to parlor tricks to make the session more interesting and were exposed as fakes. The truth of the matter is that just because people want to get together and have a séance does not mean all of the Good Spirits are willing. Sometimes the group of people does not have good harmony and this will keep the Good Spirits away. Other times, the concentration level might not be high enough to summon the proper energy. With a good Medium almost every séance will work. The Medium is the go-between of the two worlds. Some Mediums use oracles, while others simply channel the information.

One very popular technique used by Mediums is called automatic writing. The Medium can allow the spirit to enter the body and take complete control of the hand, or the Medium can receive the communication via clairaudio and simply write the information. The safest method is via clairaudio. Whenever a person allows a spirit to enter their body, there is always the risk of a bad spirit entering and taking possession. The soul of the Medium can also become trapped with another spirit. There is a term, *walk-ins,* which means to have an experienced spirit enter another person's body and take it over. Some walk-ins are positive experiences and others are absolutely dangerous. The Medium should always surround herself with a blue aura for protection before undergoing any kind of spirit communication.

The Medium is always the conductor of the séance. This does not mean that no one else can ask questions. The people in the circle around the Medium are the Sitters. These people are responsible for holding the concentrated energy. Without this energy, the spirit would not be able to communicate as easily. The Medium is the open channel and the Sitters are the electricity. It is important for all hands to be accounted for during the séance. This discourages any parlor tricks. People's hands do not have to be joined, but they do need to be flat on the table. It does not really matter what kind of table is used. Folding tables are best for table tipping (this is where the energy of the spirit raises the table and tips it).

Photographs during a séance are always interesting. Sometimes a murky substance can show on the film, which seems to come from the Medium or the Sitters. It attaches itself to any orifice of these people. This murky substance is called ectoplasm. It is a psychic energy that can take the form of a spirit.

Many ghosts and spirits have been photographed. Only one photographer should be permitted to take pictures during a séance. The photographer does not have to be in the circle of Sitters and should be permitted to photograph at any angle. A photographer is not necessary in a séance.

The room for the séance can be either fully lit or lit by candles. It should never be absolutely dark. The Sitters should always keep their eyes open, while the Medium usually closes her eyes. If the Medium is a Witch, a cleansing ritual should be done before the séance begins. The circle should not have any voices other than the Medium's when summoning the spirits. The Medium will open the circle to questions when the time is right. Since the séance is not a ritual, the Quadrant Angels and the Goddess and God are not called in. The Medium will first call in the Controller. This is usually an advanced Good Spirit with whom the Medium has had previous good experiences. The Controller is able to connect the Medium to the spirit of her choice. The Controller acts like the operator at the telephone company. After the Controller has been called, the spirit of choice is then called. The spirit of choice should be agreed upon by all participants of the séance before it begins. After the communication has been established, the Sitters may ask any important questions they choose. In all, a séance should last about an hour. By that time the Medium is usually exhausted and in need of a break.

Before adjourning the séance, the Medium should thank the Controller as well as the Good Spirit who has communicated with them. Courtesy is a must in the spirit world. If another séance is to be started after a break, it is advised that a different Medium be designated. It is also highly unlikely any group will receive the same spirit of choice for the next séance, so another spirit should be selected before the séance begins. The energy of the spirits is greatly weakened after a séance or any type of communication.

Séance Example

Select a day or night during the waxing phase of the Moon. The waxing phase ensures positive communication. If an experienced Medium is unavailable, one person must be appointed Medium to make sure the communication stays on track. Only one person talking at a time is a must. The Sitters should sit in a closed circle to enclose and protect the energy. The level of concentration should be set by everyone's meditative breathing and forming a blue aura around the entire group. The séance begins when the Medium calls the Controller.

An example of what a Medium might say: "We call upon the Spirit World to open to us now. We ask for the Good Spirit of _____ to speak to us. Part the clouds of Heaven, so she may ascend to our meeting. We await your presence. Give us a sign you are here with us."

The participants should hold total concentration until there is a sign: a rapping, an appearance, a voice, wind movement, and so forth. These are all positive signs that the Controller is present.

When the sign has been acknowledged, the Medium then continues with summoning whatever spirit the group has chosen. If the group would like to communicate with an unidentified spirit living in the house, this is permitted. The group has to have a purpose for the meeting and should not try aimless attempts to reach just any spirit.

The Medium continues: "We call upon the Spirit of _____. We ask the Controller to provide her with a path to this meeting. Hear our call. We ask for the Spirit of _____ to join our meeting."

The group waits until there is confirmation of another spirit. If there is a long silence, the group must wait. The Medium must keep the concentrated efforts alive by chanting or reasking for the spirit to appear. The Medium may say:

> Spirits compelled to enter the Round,
> Dwell within this Energy Bound.
> We call the Power to open the Gate,
> Join us in this Earthly Fate.

The Medium may say this over and over until the chosen spirit appears or communicates in some way. The circle is to remain unbroken throughout the entire séance. If the spirit is to communicate via rapping, the Medium is responsible for setting the rules: once for no, twice for yes. The Sitters may take turns in asking questions, but the Medium is to stay completely tuned in to the needs of the spirit. Communication time is usually short, so only the most important questions should be asked. The Medium may repeat the call to the spirit or repeat the rule for the rapping at any time during the séance. Fear is not an option during séances. All participants must be mentally and emotionally stable. Séances are not for everyone, and they are not to be considered entertainment.

How to Do Automatic Writing

1. Align and open all of the chakras.
2. Wear loose and comfortable clothing. Have plenty of paper and many different pens available, in case the ink runs out. Be relaxed and calm.
3. Light one yellow candle and burn Vision incense.
4. Surround yourself in a blue aura for protection.
5. Do meditative breathing.
6. Start with a prayer:

   Good Angels and Good Spirits who dwell among us, I ask that you come to me with voice and message from the Highest Existence. I ask for information to be of direct and positive nature. This is my will, So Mote It Be.

7. Write down your first question.
8. The answer that comes through must be written down immediately. Do not bother to stop the flow of information by crossing the Ts or dotting the Is. All of these things, including punctuation, should be added at the very end when the communication is over.
9. Continue asking important questions until the communication grows weak.
10. Close the communication with thanks to the *writer,* whether it be a Good Angel or Good Spirit. Say a prayer of thanks to the surrounding Good Angels and Good Spirits for their assistance.

Dark Forces

The Angels and the Good Spirits are always available to aid the Witch in all magickal endeavors. The reverse side of this coin is the negative energies existing in this world. There are low spirits who have negative intentions and also demons who involve themselves in people's lives. Their purpose is never positive and almost always destructive. There is always a purpose to their meddling, though it is not always revealed.

A black spirit can disrupt lives. Many haunted houses contain this type of energy. Perhaps it is the soul of an atheist or someone who was consumed with his own black heart. The energy is dark, depressing, and morbid. Only people who have similar qualities can hear these dark spirits. Suicide often occurs because of these black spirits. These black spirits encourage certain depressed souls to become just like them. Unfortunately, their numbers are increasing. The saying "misery loves company" is an eternal mistake.

The negative energies that interfere with people are rarely summoned. However, there are portholes in people's lives that will allow these energies to enter. The porthole is a weakness. Sometimes it is actually the structure or home allowing this energy in, but most of the time, it is a person who unintentionally allows this energy through. A ghost is not necessarily a negative energy. It is true that some ghosts are negative, but most are simply lost souls.

Demons are evil spirits spawned from hell. Demons can cause hauntings, but they are mainly interested in destroying individuals. Demons can actually possess a person's body. The person's soul is usually still in the body but is helpless in ridding the demon. A demon can possess a house or even an animal, but its main target is people. The reason demons focus on people is to obtain their souls. Demons do not usually focus on the black-hearted, but rather on the half-hearted. These people can be torn either way. The totally pure of heart are never conquests for demons. In fact, they are what threaten demons the most. In the power struggle between good and evil, the good will always win.

As there are seven levels to Heaven, there are six levels of hell. Just as there are seven different types of Angels, there are also six different types of demons. The levels of hell will range from the damnation area people can still escape from, to the lowest level that is closest to Satan. The six different types of demons are: Lucifer's winged demons, the demons who influence world leaders and people of power, the incubus, the succubus, the possessing demons, and finally the psychic attack demons.

An incubus is a demon taking the form of a human male who sexually dominates females until they surrender their soul to Satan. The succubus is a demon taking the form of a human female and seducing males until they surrender their soul to Satan. Weird sexual twists are almost always involved in the work of any demon. When demons receive sex from humans, they automatically possess their soul for eternity. Orgies can give the demons incredible power and the sex always results in a painful experience.

Clearing and Exorcism

A clearing is the depossession of a house/home. The possession can be caused by anything from a harmless ghost to demons. A clearing is a ritual that every good Witch needs to know to remove unwanted energy.

An exorcism is the depossession of a person. The term can include the depossessing of a house, but it is more often used in relation to people. An exorcism is a ritual to remove evil energies. The difference between clearings and exorcisms is mainly the intensity of the evil that is attached. An exorcism is necessary to remove the tremendous evil energy caused by demons.

It has been discovered that people with multiple personalities can be possessed by entities or demons. Of course, the medical profession totally downplays these findings, but they have been documented nonetheless. When these people were placed under hypnosis, the entity or demon was revealed and so was the intent of the possession. Some medical doctors have actually pleaded with these entities to leave and have found some of their patients cured.

When dealing with demons in either hauntings or possessions, be firm and demanding. Demons are tricky and they can sense fear, which gives them power as well as provides them with information. The power of the Goddess and the God is all you will need to remove the demon. Fear is a normal reaction, but you must overcome all fear when dealing with demons. Believe in the power of the Goddess and the God and accept nothing less.

There are not many religions that offer exorcisms. In the Catholic Church the possessed person has to manifest all the symptoms of possession before help will be considered. When the possession intensifies to that level, it is harder to exorcise the demon. The name of the Catholic exorcism is *Rituale Romanum,* which was created in 1614 A.D. A good Witch should help any deserving person, if it is within her capabilities. Some Witches may charge for services in healings, clearings, and exorcisms, while others do not. This is a personal choice. In all cases, be safe, be smart, and be persistent.

How to Do a Clearing on a Home

This should be performed on the Waning Moon, preferably on Saturday at the Saturn hour.

TOOLS   Mix together salt, pepper, garlic, lilac, mint, basil, marjoram, rosemary, and sage and place in a mojo. Consecrate some holy water. Bring a sack of onions and a small quantity of basil. Form a circle of salt for the inhabitants to stand inside of while the clearing is taking place. Burn Banishing incense and anoint each room with Protection oil.

Find the heart of the house. Start in this area and place some of the herbs there. Call upon the Quadrants to protect all four directions of the heart. Call upon the Goddess and the God to send the Light for the unprocessed spirit. Go into each room of the house. If possible, go around the house in a widdershins motion as well going around the room widdershins, and sprinkle the herbs in the corners of every room. Recite:

> With the sacred purity of Goddess and God water, I cleanse this house from all astral energies. You are not wanted here. You have no purpose, you have no life. You must now surrender into the Light. The Goddess and the God await you. The life you had no longer exists and you must leave this plane of existence. Go into the Light and find peace with your Maker. This is our will, So

Mote It Be. (Sprinkle the four corners of each room with holy water.)

Leave half of an onion in the rooms with the strongest energies. Fill the rooms with music, television, and noise. Create sound in each and every room. Before you leave the house, burn basil with Banishing incense at the front door.

How to Do an Exorcism

TOOLS   Twelve white candles, salt, water bowl, consecrated water, Exorcism incense and oil, the Holy Bible, and a rosary.

INSTRUCTIONS   Light the twelve candles and place them in a circle around the afflicted. Have the afflicted bound and laying flat. Light the incense. (It is important to keep the candles lit throughout the ceremony. Have matches ready if the candles blow out.)

Do the salt and water consecration and cleanse the magick circle. Sprinkle a heavy circle of just salt around the afflicted. Recite:

Within this magick circle is the purity of the Goddess and the God. No evil is permitted to enter this circle.

With the consecrated water (holy water) sprinkle the afflicted and say:

With this holy water, I baptize thee.

Sprinkle the afflicted again and say:

With this holy water, I cleanse thee.

Sprinkle the afflicted again and say:

With this holy water, I sanctify thee.

With the holy water make the sign of the cross over the heart of the afflicted. Recite:

In the name of the Holy Trinities: The Father, the Son, the Holy Spirit and the Maiden, the Mother, and the Crone, I cast thee evil demon out of this body and into the pits of hell from which thou came.

With the Exorcism oil anoint the feet, stomach, palms, and temples of the afflicted. The effect will feel like a burning to the demon.

Lay the rosary upon the chest of the afflicted. Open the Holy Bible to Matthew 4:10:

> Then Jesus said unto the Devil, "Get thee hence, Satan, for it is written, thou shall worship the Lord thy God and Him only shall thou serve."

Say to the demon in a loud and commanding voice:

> Thou demon of hell, you have no power here. I cast thee out of this mortal body and command you return no more. By the holy powers of the Sacred Trinities, I cast thee back into the darkness of Hell and out of this mortal body. You no longer have will, for the powers of Christ compel you. The powers of Christ compel you. The powers of Christ compel you.

Anoint with Exorcism oil on the forehead of the afflicted, the sign of the cross. Recite:

> This is the temple of the Goddess and the God. There is no evil permitted to touch this body.

Watch for signs of release from the demon. Recite:

> The twelve candles represent the disciples of Christ. You are surrounded by the holy presence.

If the demon is still within the body, proceed with invoking the Quadrants and the Angels. Call upon the presence of the Goddess and the God. Recite:

> The powers of goodness surround you. Your power is gone and you cannot stay within this mortal body. Out with you, demon of darkness!

If the demon has not left, recite the Twenty-Third Psalm over and over. If the demon is still not gone, do not release the Quadrants or thank the Goddess and God until it has been released. The magick circle is not to be broken until the demon is gone.

CEREM⊕NIAL RITES

For the couple a day to wed,
For the female first day she bled.
For the birthing a day to bless,
For the dying a day to rest.
All within the Wiccan rite,
Share the seasons of the life.
Tears for joy and tears for sorrow,
Cherish today and tomorrow.
For every love there is a season,
For every pain there is reason.
For every beat that rhymes the heart,
For every light there is dark.
The Witches will gather, rejoice, and sing,
To all the rites that life will bring.
The Witches will circle when life must end,
To cross it over and then transcend.

BELLADONNA

A good Witch will celebrate numerous Sabbats and Esbats throughout the year, but there are also other important days involving ceremonies. These special days are weddings, births, and passovers. All of these special events have a Wiccan tradition that is still alive and well.

There is always the question of mixed marriages, which needs to be addressed. A mixed marriage is one involving two different religions. Does a Wiccan marriage mean the other person must become a Wiccan? The answer is no. A couple may indeed have a mixed marriage with any religious ceremony they choose. Remember, Wiccans never convert people to their religion. If, however, a woman is Wiccan and the man is anti-Goddess/God and believes in no other universal power than himself, then not only is he foolish, but he is not permitted to have any Wiccan ceremony whatsoever. The same holds true for anyone who does not have purity of heart—there will be no ritual of any kind wasted on these individuals.

A good Witch will never recommend these ceremonies for anyone outside of the Wiccan religion—not even if it is for a close friend who desires some kind of New Age, groovy, funky-kind-of-stuff wedding. These ceremonies derive from an ancient tradition and are only for those who truly worship as we do.

Witches are festive beings, but the purpose of these ceremonies is to obtain true spiritual blessings in our lives. The Goddess and God approving of our choices and blessing our lives makes this lifetime worth living.

Handfast

A Handfast is a sacred marriage ceremony between two Wiccans. Handfasts can be either legal or nonlegal ceremonies, depending on the preference of the couple. One example of this is two people who are gay and want to be married. As of this date, it is illegal for two gay people to marry. So, while other religions do not support gay marriages, the Wiccans believe that any two people, no matter what their sexual orientation, have the right to marry. Some Wiccans may choose to marry, but would rather skip the legalities and hold true to the vows just the same. The couple has the right to choose whether the wedding is to be legal or nonlegal.

The High Priestess is always the one to conduct any Wiccan ceremony. The High Priest is sometimes invited to be the co-conductor of the ceremonies. Between the High Priestess and High Priest, one of these two has usually been ordained by the Universal Life Church in California and is able to perform any ceremony legally. Because of this, any traditional wedding extras can be added, including the marriage license.

Most Handfasts are legal ceremonies. If the couple chooses to have a Handfast without the legalities, even the High Priestess may be optioned out. The couple may perform their own ceremony with just the Goddess and God, and that is all that is necessary.

The Handfast can be shared with or without witnesses. Handfasts are always on the waxing side of the Moon or the Full Moon. The time of day or night is completely optional, as long as the ceremony begins on the half-hour. The reason for this is to ensure that luck is sweeping upward toward the hour.

Most Handfasts take place outdoors in natural surroundings. This type of a Handfast feels very comfortable to everyone. An old tree stump will make a nice altar, decorated with fresh flowers and magickal stones. It is also nice to have indoor Handfasts, but the outdoor ones are my favorites. The feeling is somehow closer to the Goddess and God.

Most Handfasts will last about thirty minutes. Generally, the couple will insist upon audience participation through the whole ceremony. I believe that rehearsing the Handfast is necessary because it seems to flow smoother and feel more relaxed. It is a beautiful ceremony that is also quite serious. After the ceremony the festivities are always fun.

A magickal circle should be cast with a nine-foot radius. The altar and the wedded couple should stand inside this circle. The family and close friends should be seated in a circle around the couple. Acquaintances and coworkers should make a third circle farther out, and so on. The coven members should create the last and final circle around the Handfast area. The coven members will link hands and never let the circle be broken. This is the Ring of Protection.

If the Handfast calls for the High Priest to co-conduct, the bride and the High Priestess should stand with their backs to the North and West, respectively. The groom and the High Priest should stand with their backs to the South and East, respectively. If the Handfast calls for the High Priestess alone to do the ceremony, the bride stands to the North and the groom stands to the South. The High Priestess stands to the West.

The apparel of the bride may range from a formal wedding gown to skyclad. A laurel for the hair is usually worn instead of a veil. The bride's gown is usually white and simple. The bouquet is always made of fresh flowers. The apparel of the groom will vary as well. The groom will wear a flower on his garment and also attach a mojo bag of magickal herbs to his Wiccan cingula. He may also wear a laurel for his head, but this is optional.

The incense may vary, but Myrrh is often chosen. The ritual oil will vary as well, but Handfast is favored. The nine-foot circle where the ceremony will take place should be marked with rose petals. The cord that binds the couple should be prepared months before the Handfast. It should be jointly made by the bride and groom. All sorts of materials can be used to make this cord, but it should be woven or braided and made with three different colors. The color white should be one of the selected colors. Flowers and vines may also be used in the cord.

A wedding party of ushers and bridesmaids can be added. The participants can range from no one to everyone. The Handfast should be designed to make the wedded couple happy.

The wine that is offered to the guests should be both white and red. The bride should pour the red and the groom should pour the white. The post-ceremony wedding should be whatever the couple decides on. Some Handfasts will include a toast from everyone present.

Live music is best for this type of occasion, but recorded music is the next best. Singing and dancing are always included. The music for the ceremony is selected to mean something special to the bride and groom.

The final tradition to the Handfast is jumping over the broom. This signifies jumping into life. Another tradition is jumping over a fire. One or the other is done. When the jump is complete, the guests should stand and shout, "So Mote It Be!"

The Ceremony

A ritual bath should be taken the morning of the ceremony. The bride and groom should not see each other before the wedding ceremony. The ritual bath allows personal time to reflect upon the vows and the commitment ahead.

Prepare the altar. Begin the music. Light the incense and Unity candle.

The High Priestess cleanses the circle, casts the circle, calls the Quadrants and invokes the Goddess and God.

The High Priestess says:

> We come into this world with our eyes wide open. Not knowing exactly what is ahead of us, but trusting that love will provide us with all we need. We come to this magick circle with our eyes wide open. The two people before you today do not know what life

has in store for them, but they trust love will provide them with all they need. We have come together in celebration to witness the union of two hearts. We are seated in the garden of the Goddess in the midst of her beautiful creation, to celebrate the commitment these two people have made. Who stands beside you in your decision of marriage?

The best man and the matron of honor respond together:

We do.

They are then seated in the inner circle.
High Priestess:

How do you come to this magick circle?

Bride and Groom together:

With perfect love and perfect trust.

High Priestess:

(Groom's name), do you promise to give perfect love and perfect trust to your wife? In this pledge, do you promise to let her grow, and will you nurture her and comfort her whenever she needs?

Groom responds:

Yes, I will.

High Priestess:

(Bride's name), do you promise to give perfect love and perfect trust to your husband? In this pledge, do you promise to let him grow, and will you nurture him and comfort him whenever he needs?

Bride responds:

Yes, I will.

High Priestess:

Do you have the emotional support from a loving family who will help you during the difficult times and will always love you as you will always love them?

The family responds:

Yes, they have our love and support.

High Priestess:

*This magick circle contains a continual flow of love. You have
been surrounded by Angels, the Goddess and God, and all of these
people who love you. I now cast another circle enclosing just the
two of you.* (With the athame, the High Priestess draws a
circle around the two of them.) *Within your magick circle there
is perfect love. Within the outer magick circle, there is perfect love
also. Both circles have no beginning and no end, just as your love
is for one another. What symbols have you chosen to signify your
love?*

Bride and Groom:

We offer these rings.

High Priestess:

*These rings are blessed by all of the powers of the universe. They
have been submerged in the Earth to ground your love. They have
been passed through Air to lift your spirits. They have been passed
through Fire to warm your hearts. They have been submerged in
Water to cleanse your soul. Raphael. Michael. Gabriel. Uriel.
Bless these symbols of love.*

The Groom places the ring on the Bride's finger, and the Bride
places the ring on the Groom's finger.

The High Priestess hands the cake to the Groom. As the Groom
feeds a piece of cake to the Bride he says:

*I promise you will never hunger for love. I will feed all of your
desires with every ounce of my soul.*

The High Priestess hands the chalice to the Bride. She holds the
chalice for the Groom to take a drink and says:

*I promise you will never thirst for love. I will quench all of your
desires with every ounce of my soul.*

High Priestess:

In the garden of Eden is where Adam met Eve. In this garden of the Goddess is where (Bride's name) *and* (Groom's name) *became as one. In honor of this commitment, we offer you three flowers. The first flower will blossom with respect. The second flower will blossom with kindness. The third flower will blossom with trust. With these flowers, your garden will always flourish with love.*

The Bride and Groom then exchange the personal vows they have written for each other.

High Priestess:

Within this union of two hearts, you are hereby bound together by your promise of love. Witnessed within this garden of the Goddess on this _____ (number) day of _____ (month), _____ (year). (The High Priestess ties the Bride's and Groom's hands together with their cord.) *In the presence of the Towers, the Goddess and God, and all these people here today, we now marry you to each other and bless this sacred union with happiness. You are now handfasted from here to eternity. All of those in favor, say: So Mote It Be!*

All say:

So Mote It Be!

The Bride and Groom, still bound together, jump over the broom. The High Priestess dismisses the Quadrants, and thanks the Goddess and God. All adjourn to festivities.

The Great Rite

The Great Rite, also known as the Rite to Union, is a sacred and unifying act performed by the Bride and Groom after the Handfast ceremony. It is a ritual, including a sexual consummation of the body and soul.

The Great Rite should take as much planning as the Handfast. There should be no one else present during this ceremony. It can be performed indoors or outdoors, as long as the couple has complete privacy. The altar for the Great Rite should be set prior to the ceremony.

The Great Rite is a powerful ritual. It is done in remembrance of the divine union of the Goddess and God. It is to remind us all that life will always continue because of the love and physical union we share.

The Ceremony

Prepare an altar with a red cloth for the base, two candles representing the Goddess and God, incense with the combination of Handfast and Blessed Be, and the chalice.

The husband lights the God candle.

The wife lights the Goddess candle.

The husband lights the incense.

The wife pours the red wine into the chalice.

The husband invokes the Quarters with the athame, saying:

> *I call upon the Towers of the East.*
> *I call upon the Towers of the South.*
> *I call upon the Towers of the West.*
> *I call upon the Towers of the North.*
> *I invoke thee Towers to preside this night,*
> *To embrace and bless our union for this Great Rite.*

The wife now invokes the Goddess and God:

> *I call upon Goddess, creator of wives.*
> *I call upon God, creator of husbands.*
> *Join us in ceremony and celebration.*
> *This Rite to Union is dedicated to Thee.*

The wife and husband now pledge a promise to each other that will be kept at all cost. The husband makes his pledge first while the wife holds the chalice for him to drink. Then the wife makes her pledge while the husband holds the chalice for her to drink (the wine seals the pledge). They now enjoy sexual intercourse with patience and love. This is where their souls mix and become as one. After the Great Rite has been consummated, the husband releases the Towers:

> To the South, North, West, and East.
> With gratitude and praise, you are released.

The wife then thanks the Goddess and God:

> To the mighty Goddess and God in flight,
> We thank you for joining us in this Great Rite.
> So Mote It Be.

Snuff out the Goddess and God candles.

The Sacred Rite

The Sacred Rite anniversary ritual is a ceremony reminding us of the marriage vows that were once taken, and to add to those vows the new feelings that have occurred during the marriage. It is a time to release and forgive past issues of the marriage, and to make new efforts and promises to improve the marriage.

The Ceremony

The altar should be set directly across from the area where sexual intercourse will take place. The altar should include the Goddess and God candles, the athame, the chalice, and a wedding cake. The altar should be set with a red cloth; it should also have a picture of the wedding day or any other memory of the wedding day. The place where sexual intercourse will take place should be sprinkled with rose petals. Cleanse the circle.

The husband invokes the Quadrants:

> Spirits of the East, we summon.
> Join us in this private coven.
> Spirits of the South, we compel.
> Join us in this marriage spell.

Spirits of the West, please ascend.
Join us in this fest again.
Spirits of the North, all unite.
Join us in this Sacred Rite.

The wife summons the Goddess and God:

Lady of the Moon and Lord of the Sun,
Empower us now and make us one.

The husband and wife now read to each other their original marriage vows. They talk about the wedding day and all of the events that have happened since then. The husband and wife write new vows fitting the way they feel now and read them to each other. This is the time to forgive past situations and talk about a strategy to improve their marriage.

The husband cuts a piece of the Sacred Rite cake and says:

This cake represents my body. I will always feed you with love and kindness.

The wife now cuts a piece of the Sacred Rite cake and says:

This cake represents my body. I will always feed you with love and kindness.

The wife pours the wine and holds the chalice for her husband to drink. She says:

This is my blood that flows with the motion of perpetual love and kindness.

The husband now holds the chalice for his wife to drink and says:

This is my blood that flows with the motion of perpetual love and kindness.

Sexual intercourse takes place with patience and tenderness. The husband then dismisses the Quadrants:

To the mighty Towers with all their powers,
Thank you for joining us in this magickal hour.

The wife gives gratitude to the Goddess and God:

To the Goddess and God, we adjourn with respect.
Thankful for love and all that you protect.
So Mote It Be.

Handpart

A Handparting is the Wiccan divorce. This is when the pagan couple has tried everything to make their marriage work, but to no avail. Most Wiccans are strong and dedicated people. They do not end marriages because of trivial disagreements or lack of effort. The Wiccan marriage ends when the couple has tried every way possible to have happiness between them. When their efforts of reconciliation are exhausted, the Handparting is necessary.

This ceremony is not a legal divorce in the eyes of the justice system. This means a legal divorce must be filed and completed before the Handparting ritual.

The High Priestess usually conducts the ceremony. The High Priest is sometimes invited to be co-conductor. The other option to this ceremony is for the divorcing couple to perform it by themselves. It is usually better to have the High Priestess perform the ceremony.

The coven or any other witnesses may attend if the couple asks them to. If the coven does attend, they link hands in a circle and form a Ring of Protection. The time of a Handparting is at sunset during a waning moon. Most pick Saturday as the day for this ceremony, as it is the day of endings.

The altar for the High Priestess to use is covered with a black cloth. The usual tools and candles will be used except the Unity candle. Instead of using a white candle, a black candle is used. The other additions to the altar are a copy of the marriage license and a copy of the divorce decree (the couple should always retain their originals for their personal records). There also needs to be a copied picture of their Handfasting, a ritual cleansing oil, the cord used to bind the couple, and both wedding rings.

This is a very solemn occasion. There are no festivities. It is a time to recognize how growth has sprouted in two different paths. It is the death of promises that once were bright. This ceremony marks a time to reflect upon the past, to forgive, and to heal. The Handparting couple should wear all black and be in traditional Wiccan wardrobe.

The High Priestess cleanses the circle, casts the circle, and calls the Quadrants:

Towers and Angels of the infinite Power
Ascend to witness Handparting this hour.
Raphael, Michael, Gabriel and Uriel.
Welcome. Your presence is our honor.

The High Priestess lights the Goddess and God candles and invokes them:

Loving Lady, Mother and Crone,
Aid us in the divide of this home.
Almighty Lord, Father of Sky,
Bless us in these hands untied.

The High Priestess to the couple:

How do you present yourselves to this magick circle?

They answer:

With perfect love and perfect trust.

High Priestess:

We gather here in the presence of the Angels, the Towers, and the Lady and Lord. We gather here to part the hands that once were tied (the High Priestess lights the black candle). We ask that the Lady and Lord will grant this Handparting with their blessing. We ask for dissolve and parting of this once sacred union.

The couple now kneels before the altar with heads bowed.
High Priestess:

The Witch and Warlock before you present themselves.

The husband says his legal name and his Wiccan name.
The wife says her legal name and her Wiccan name.
High Priestess:

> *Their request of Handparting is to resume their lives in individual*
> *dwellings. They no longer feel the love they once shared.*

The couple stands.

The High Priestess takes the athame and draws separate circles
around each one. She then takes the athame to remove any invisible
strings or bindings that may be attached. The athame is moved
along their sides and over their heads to completely free them. As
the High Priestess does this cutting, she says:

> *I cut the binding cord from the husband. May he no longer feel*
> *burden, pain, guilt, or sorrow from this marriage. I cut the*
> *binding cord from the wife. May she no longer feel burden, pain,*
> *guilt, or sorrow from this marriage. What do you present this*
> *Circle of Truth as your offering?*

The couple responds:

> *We offer our wedding rings.*

The High Priestess puts the rings through salt, feather, Fire, and
Water. She says:

> *These rings are each grounded by Earth, lifted by Air, warmed by*
> *Fire, and cleansed by Water. These symbols of love are now free*
> *and released of their purpose. They are absolved of all negatives*
> *and are no longer symbols of this union. You are free to do with*
> *these whatever you wish.*

The High Priestess hands them each their rings. She holds copies
of the marriage license and divorce decree. She cleanses and anoints
them. She holds up the marriage license and says:

> *Lady and Lord. Forgive this couple, as only you can. We also ask*
> *you to place forgiveness in their hearts for each other. This*
> *marriage is now released.*

The High Priestess burns the license in the black candle and says:

From ashes to ashes, this union is now divided.

The High Priestess holds up the divorce decree and says:

Lady and Lord. We pray you accept this dividing with your blessing.

The High Priestess burns the divorce decree from the black candle and says:

From dust to dust, it is now done.
So Mote It Be.

The High Priestess now takes scissors and cuts the couple apart from the wedding picture. She then cuts the cord that once bound them together, into two pieces. She says:

The Goddess and the God have given their permission and blessing to this Handparting. The bond you once shared is now a memory. The new journey before you begins. Your marriage is now dissolved and you are separate individuals. The new names that are legally known to the world are _____ and _____. We pray these individuals are now wiser and happier for having had this experience in life.

The High Priestess snuffs out the black candle and says:

All in favor of this Handparting.

All members say:

So Mote It Be.

The High Priestess dismisses the Quadrants:

To the Governing Angels and Their source, We thank you for your loving support.

The High Priestess thanks the Goddess and God:

To the Lady and Lord of Love and Light, We thank you for this Handparting Rite. So Mote It Be.

The liberated female opens the circle.

Birthing Rite

A Birthing Rite is a ceremony celebrating the birth of a child. There are two different types of Birth Rites: one is known as the Circle of Life and the other is the Blessing. The difference between the two rites is that the Circle of Life is performed for two Wiccan parents, and the Blessing is for a baby of any religion.

The Circle of Life is a planned ceremony with the intent of performing the ritual after the birth of the baby. One important component for this ritual is the afterbirth. The ceremony should be held on the first full moon after the baby is born. A small fruit tree is needed for this event. Dig a hole large enough for planting the tree. First the afterbirth will be placed in the hole, then the tree. The mother will hold the infant while the father braces the tree. The High Priestess and coven are present for this occasion.

The Circle of Life

The High Priestess cleanses the circle, then casts the circle saying:

Blessed be the husband and wife,
And the blessed infant to whom they gave life.
Blessed by all the powers above,
Conceived in perfect trust and love.

All coven members join hands in a circle around the tree, including the mother, father, and baby. Dance in a clockwise motion.

The High Priestess calls the Quadrants:

Raphael, Michael, Gabriel, and Uriel!
A celebration requires your presence.
East, South, West, and North,
Assemble with all of your essence.

The High Priestess calls the Goddess and God:

Blessed Lord and Lady Divine,
We ask that you join this Circle of Life.

> Bless this infant with your infinite grace,
> Bless this family and this holy place.

All stop dancing.
High Priestess:

> In this holy place, life is conceived. The pulse of life is now offered
> to this tree. (Place the afterbirth in the hole.) This blessed child
> will never hunger, for it will always be fed with this eternal fruit of
> life. (Place consecrated water in the hole.) This blessed child will
> never thirst, for it will always receive water from this eternal
> source of life. (Place fingernail clippings from the infant in the
> hole.) I offer this gift from the blessed infant. This is to give life to
> life. We pray the infant will have a strong and musical voice to
> sing praises to the Goddess and God. (Place tree into hole.) Three
> gifts of life for life itself. We pray the Goddess and God will bless
> this child with three special gifts as well. (Father now holds child
> up to the heavens.) We pray the Lady and Lord will bless this
> life, which has given joy to all who are near her. (Father and
> mother both cradle the infant while the High Priestess anoints
> the third eye with holy water.) In the name of the holy trinities:
> the Father, the Son, and the Holy Spirit; the Maiden, the Mother,
> and the Crone. I offer blessings to thee, precious infant, may you
> never know pain, suffering, or hunger. But rather you only know
> love, honesty, trust, and laughter. Bless this family. Give strength to
> this baby. Bless this life. And so it is and So Mote It Be!

All say:

> So Mote It Be!

The High Priestess gives the parents a bouquet of flowers for the
infant and says:

> May this always remind you of how precious life is.

The parents are to hang the bouquet near the bassinet and when
the flowers start to die, hang them to dry and press them into a
baby book.

The High Priestess dismisses the Quadrants:

With praise and gratitude in all our best,
To the North, South, East, and West.

The High Priestess thanks the Goddess and God:

Lord of Light, Lady of Love,
We thank the Powers of all above.

The High Priestess opens the circle.

The Blessing

To be performed on the first Full Moon after the baby's birth. A small altar setting is needed, as well as a fresh bouquet of flowers. The High Priestess is the only person required, but the coven can attend if the parents wish. The High Priestess cleanses the circle, calls the Quadrants, and calls the Goddess and God. She waves the small bouquet over the baby's head and says:

Precious Lamb of Angels' delight.
Bless this child from morn till night.
Keep her safe, happy, and warm.
Bless this day this child was born.
Guide her to the paths of light.
Bless her with the inner sight.
Let happiness grow where she abounds.
Keep her feet close to the sacred ground.
May she listen to the Angels for when they speak.
To feel inner strength when the flesh is weak.
Bless her with knowledge of heaven, Goddess, and God.
Bless this child, may she grow in love.

The parents hang the small bouquet over the bassinet out of the baby's reach. When the flowers start to die, the parents should dry and press them into a baby book.

High Priestess offers a benediction:

To all of those with purity of heart, till next we merry meet and
merry part. So Mote It Be.

High Priestess dismisses the Quadrants:

With praise and gratitude in all our best,
To the North, South, East, and West.

High Priestess thanks the Goddess and God:

Lord of Light, Lady of Love,
We thank the Powers of all above.

The High Priestess opens the circle.

Coming of Age

When our babies grow up and start to resemble young men and women, we realize the Goddess is fulfilling the cycles of life again. We are no longer new mothers, but rather the mothers of young adults. The rules in mothering change slightly. No longer is it easy to take candy from the baby. Our children's minds are sharp and full of questions. We need to deal with their questions honestly and with tact.

When my youngest child approached me with the question, "Mommy, what is a virgin?" the question hit me like a ton of bricks. I wondered where she had heard the word and figured it must have been on television. My response to her was: "A virgin is someone who has never had sexual relations before. It is something everyone should be very proud of. It means their body is a temple of the Goddess and it is not to be shared with anyone else until there are feelings of love that are mutually expressed with another person. It is a sacred time of life when purity of the soul speaks to the heart. Virginity is something so special some people choose to keep it sacred forever."

Her next question was, "Mommy, am I a virgin?" My heart was so touched by the innocence of the question I had to choke back tears. I said, "Of course, you are. You are as pure as the new-fallen snow." She seemed very satisfied with that answer. Then she asked me, "Mommy, are you a virgin?" After a brief pause I said, "Of course, I am." Goddess, please forgive me. I promise to tell her the truth by the time she is ten.

The ritual for our children to acknowledge their biological and mental changes is called Maidens of Season for the girls and Masters of Sun for the boys. The boys will have their ritual at age thirteen. That is when they should be acknowledged as young men. The girls will have their ritual the first full moon after they begin their menstrual cycle.

The rituals for each are very special but do not involve the High Priestess or the coven. They simply involve the parents and their children. The girls should have this ritual with their mothers and boys with their fathers. If, however, there is only one parent, that one has the responsibility of performing this ritual.

This is a special day for both you and your child. There should be no one else participating in these rituals, such as another child who could distract you. This day is for your child, who has become a young adult, and is a celebration of that fact. The ritual can be lengthy, as long as three to four hours. Be sure you have planned enough time so there will be no interruptions.

Maidens of Season

Due to the fact you cannot exactly predict the day your daughter will begin her first period, you should at least be aware of her physical and emotional changes. This way you can be somewhat prepared for when the day arrives. You should tell your daughter that the two of you will share something very special on that day (the first Full Moon after she starts menstruating), so she can get excited about it. This is really a celebration and not a dreaded curse. On the first Full Moon after your daughter starts her cycle:

You should start by telling your daughter how proud you are of her and how exciting it is to become a woman. The physical changes are obvious at this point, but the emotional changes may not be so obvious to her. Make her aware of her feelings and also of her psychic and intuitive abilities. She should be able to have a sense of what is happening to her. Make her aware of mood shifts and her sensory areas. She needs to be able to completely understand woman's intuition.

This will be an unusual shopping day for the two of you. The craft or fabric store is the first place to start. You will need to create her first poppet. Find a pattern for a simple rag doll. Buy all the materials to make this doll complete. When you get home, show your daughter how to start creating this doll. Cut out the fabric, sew the main seams, and create an outfit for the doll. When you get to the point where you are ready to stuff the doll, you should create a special mojo for its insides. Inside the mojo is a secret letter you have written for her to have for the rest of her life. This is a keepsake she will pass on to her children. Included with the letter, there should be special stones, herbs, or magick you have selected for this occasion to ensure her long life, happiness, and good health. She is permitted to read the letter before it is placed in the mojo and then sealed inside the doll. Complete the entire doll with her and tell her that whenever she feels sad, she is suppose to get this doll and tell it all of her problems. Be sure to give the doll a name. Tell her the magick inside the doll will make things better.

When the doll is complete, consecrate it, suffumigate it, and anoint it. The doll is now complete, just like the cycle of childhood.

Masters of Sun

When boys have approached their thirteenth birthday, they have reached the threshold of manhood. The father is the most appropriate person to aid the child in this ritual, but mothers will also do. This is a time to discuss how the physical body changes and matures. It is time to talk about why boys need to treat girls with respect and gentleness.

On this special day, get away from the city lights and go out into nature. A long hike in the woods or mountains is perfect for this day. Blaze new trails and discuss how your ancestors had to live by the laws of Nature. Pay attention to the season, the time of day, and the smell of the air. Make sure your son is aware of his surroundings.

While out in the midst of nature, find a tall walking stick. Try to find one that is very close to the height of your son. Make sure it is a naturally fallen branch so you do not have to cut one from a tree.

Be sure the stick is strong and thick. As you are walking along, hopefully you will find a body of water. Stand near the water's edge and consecrate the stick, first for purity and then for power. Be sure to carry water with you in case you do not find any when you are walking. Do this ritual as you believe an Indian chief would for his young brave.

At some point during your journey, take a break to sit down and carve thirteen marks into the walking stick. This will serve as a constant reminder of this special birthday. Some very talented fathers are even able to carve faces into their sticks. This walking stick is a gift to your son. Tell him to be strong and proud. Build a small fire, suffumigate the stick, and anoint it with oil. Remind your son that if ever he becomes weak and strays from the divine path, he will always have his walking stick to help him. After all, now he is a man.

Rite of Passage

A Rite of Passage is a ritual performed when a loved one is already in the dying process. It is a ceremony given by Wiccans for Wiccans and is performed by the coven to ensure safe and easy passage for the soul. It is a ceremony that involves summoning the Angels to carry the soul from this life into the next realm. It is also a time to ease any physical discomforts and to say good-bye to loved ones.

When the dying process is close, this ritual should be performed. It does not have to wait until the last few minutes of life. If death is absolutely inevitable and the person has come to terms with her death, she should arrange for the Rite of Passage. The Rite of Passage is usually requested when the person is bedridden and the cause of death is either old age or a terminal disease. This is one of the most sacred moments in any ritual work because all of the heavenly Angels are summoned and their positive powers assist you in this ceremony.

The wardrobe of the coven is full ritual attire, including the black robes. The only things omitted from the wardrobe during any passing rite are the shoes. If the ceremony is outdoors and shoes are needed for protection, then it is permissible to wear them. When the coven is convening in a person's dying chamber for the Rite of Passage, their feet must be washed and dried before entering. Absolutely no shoes are permitted in the dying chamber during this ritual.

If a Wiccan were to die unexpectedly, such as in a car accident, a full ritual known as the Circle of Destiny is to be performed. All of the coven members are required to be present, and the ceremony will take place after the family has had its ceremony. This ritual involves the summoning of the loved one to return for the final good-bye. This ceremony also summons the white Angels to carry the soul back to the heavenly mansion.

The question often arises, "What if I am not a Wiccan and I want this ceremony performed for me?" My first response would be, "Why would a person of no religion or of another religion want this rite done?" The reason people might request this is to be sure they will pass into the hands of Angels and not into the claws of the demons. People who are dying sometimes become desperate in search of an insurance policy to heaven. A ceremony may be performed for these individuals, but it is not the Rite of Passage. This particular ceremony is called a Passover. A Passover is very different from the Rite of Passage. The coven has no right to ask the Goddess and God to take this soul to heaven. The coven has the power to ask for cleansing and forgiveness of the soul. The coven also has the right to ask the Escorting Angels to greet the soul.

What if a coven member's mother is dying and the mother is a devout Catholic, but she requests a Rite of Passage? I believe that if the coven member and her mother have a close relationship based on love and respect, then this ritual may be performed. Most people will not want to cross religious lines, but for the pure of heart there are always exceptions. For those who are dying and have no purity of heart, Passovers are their only option and only if they request it. All ceremonies performed by Wiccans are done by request. There should be no volunteering to do ceremonies for anyone outside of the Wiccan religion.

For any passage ceremony use twelve white candles representing the Escorting Angels from heaven, the Goddess and God candles, and one large Unity candle. The incense may be either Frankincense or Myrrh. Salt and water are needed for consecration. A crucifix is usually placed upon the chest of the loved one during the Rite of Passage. Any anointing oil of high vibration, such as Blessed Be, can be used.

The Rite of Passage

The High Priestess will cleanse the circle, then cast the circle:

Blessed be the pure of heart,
That gather together in light or dark.
Hear our voices combine as one,
We draw the magick from moon to sun.

With background music playing, light the twelve white candles and the incense. The coven members form a circle and hold hands to contain the energy; then the High Priestess summons the Quadrants and their Angels:

Raphael.
I call upon the Eastern Towers.
Join us in this Rite of Passage.
Michael.
I call upon the Southern Towers.
Join us in this Rite of Passage.
Gabriel.
I call upon the Western Towers.
Join us in this Rite of Passage.
Uriel.
I call upon the Northern Towers.
Join us in this Rite of Passage.

The High Priestess calls the Escorting Angels of heaven:

I call upon the Angels that guard the gates of heaven. I welcome you and ask for your assistance in this Rite of Passage.

The High Priestess calls the Goddess and God. She lights the Goddess and God candles:

Loving Lady, our heavenly Mother.
I welcome you to empower this magick circle.
Almighty Lord, our heavenly Father.
I welcome you to empower this magick circle.

The High Priestess places the crucifix on the chest of the dying. All in the room recite the Twenty-Third Psalm:

The Lord is my shepherd, I shall not want. He maketh me lie down in green pastures, He leadeth me beside the still waters. He restoreth my soul. He leadeth me in the paths of righteousness for His name's sake. Yea, though I walk through the valley of the shadow of death, I will fear no evil, for Thou art with me. Thy rod and Thy staff they comfort me. Thou preparest a table before me in the presence of mine enemies. Thou anointest my head with oil. My cup runneth over. Surely goodness and mercy shall follow me all the days of my life. And I will dwell in the house of the Lord forever.

High Priestess says:

We are in a most holy place. The entities of heaven are among us. The Quadrant Angels empower us. The Goddess and God fulfill us. We have called upon these heavenly hosts to aid us in our Rite of Passage for our sister (brother) _____. As the seasons of life have changed for us, we realize the soul must now evolve and change. The body has encompassed our soul and it has served its purpose. The soul requires a time of release and though we are saddened for our loss, we rejoice in _____'s release. We ask you take this precious soul that we love and care for, to the heavenly mansion where she (he) will know the abundance of unconditional love. We ask for a safe and easy journey to this passage.

At this time, each member of the circle will make an offering. This is where a special wish has been written down on white parchment. It is burned from the Unity candle and placed into the cauldron. As each wish is burned, the member will say:

May this wish live in your heart,
For next we merry meet and merry part.
So Mote It Be.

After the last wish has been cast, the High Priestess mixes the remaining incense into the cauldron with the ashes. The High Priestess draws a pentagram on the forehead of the dying with the anointing oil. All recite:

Our Father and Mother which art in heaven.
Hallowed be Thy name.
Thy kingdom come. Thy will be done
On earth, as it is in heaven.
Give us this day our daily bread.
And forgive us of our debts, as we forgive our debtors.
And lead us not into temptation, but deliver us from evil.
For Thine is the kingdom, and the power, and the glory, forever.
So Mote It Be.

High Priestess:

We pray to our Heavenly Hosts the soul of our sister (brother)
_____ will be released during the most blessed dream. We ask
the heavenly Angels to stay with our friend from this point until
passage. We thank all the Angels and the Goddess and God for
allowing us this final time together.

The High Priestess dismisses the Quadrants:

To the North, South, East, and West.
With gratitude and praise. So be blessed.

The High Priestess thanks the Goddess and God:

Lord and Lady of almighty power,
Thank you for aiding us in this magickal hour.

All candles are extinguished except the Unity candle.
High Priestess:

> *This candle now shines of one.*
> *Our journey has now begun.*
> *This circle is now open.*
> *But Is forever, unbroken.*
> *So Mote It Be.*

The Passover

Light the ritual incense, and light three white candles. Stand in a circle around the dying person and link hands. Cleanse the circle. Background music should be playing softly.
Cast the circle:

> *Blessed be the pure of heart*
> *That gather together in light or dark.*
> *Hear our voices combine as one.*
> *We draw the magick from moon to sun.*

All recite the Twenty-Third Psalm.
High Priestess:

> *This holy water of consecration is to purify the soul.*

Make the sign of the cross on the person's forehead.
The High Priestess now holds the unity candle:

> *This is the light of forgiveness. I pray that you be absolved from all sins and I pray that you forgive those who have sinned against you. We pray in unity that the Angels of heaven welcome you and give you safe passage from this life into the next.*

All recite the Lord's Prayer.
Open the circle.

The Circle of Destiny

The remains of the loved one should be at a central location. This can be at the grave site or if ashes are contained, then at any dwelling place chosen. Also, if ashes have been scattered, the outdoor area should be selected and a few belongings of the loved one should be there.

The altar should be prepared with Frankincense or Myrrh incense; three white candles representing the Goddess, God, and the Unity; chalice, athame, cauldron, bell, and pentagram; and salt and water for consecration.

The ceremony should be started on the hour.

Cleanse the circle.

The High Priestess casts the circle:

Blessed be the pure of heart
That gather together in light or dark.
Hear our voices combine as one.
We draw the magick from moon to sun.

Ring the Bell.

The High Priestess calls the Quadrants:

Raphael.
I call upon the Eastern Towers.
Join us in this Circle of Destiny.
Michael.
I call upon the Southern Towers.
Join us in this Circle of Destiny.
Gabriel.
I call upon the Western Towers.
Join us in this Circle of Destiny.
Uriel.
I call upon the Northern Towers.
Join us in this Circle of Destiny.

Ring the Bell.
The High Priestess calls the Goddess and God:

Loving Lady, our heavenly Mother.
I welcome you to empower this magick circle.
Almighty Lord, our heavenly Father.
I welcome you to empower this magick circle.

Ring the Bell.
High Priestess:

We gather here today to say good-bye to our sister (brother)
_____. We ask the soul of our loved one is able to be present
here with us today inside this Circle of Destiny. We have formed
this circle with perfect love and perfect trust. _____ we wish
you happiness, warmth, and love.

At this time, each coven member will make a verbal offering. After
the wish has been made for the loved one, a flower is placed inside
the cauldron. The High Priestess is the last one to make an offering.
Ring the Bell.
High Priestess:

To our beloved _____, we offer you these wishes. May they be
with you from here to eternity. We pray the white Angels will
escort you to the heavenly mansion. Though your physical self will
be missed by all, we know you will always be in our minds and in
our hearts. We love you.

Ring the Bell.
The coven members all raise their chalices and propose a toast as
to how they will always remember the loved one.
Ring the Bell.
The High Priestess dismisses the Quadrants:

To the North, South, East, and West.
With gratitude and praise. So be blessed.

The High Priestess thanks the Goddess and God:

Lord and Lady of Almighty Power.
Thank you for aiding us in this magickal hour.

Extinguish all candles but the Unity candle.
The High Priestess opens the circle:

This candle now shines of one.
Our journey has now begun.
This circle is now open.
But is forever, unbroken.
So Mote It Be.

If the ceremony is to be held outdoors, small white votive candles may be placed in a circle around the loved one. Make sure the area is fireproof and let the candles blow out by themselves. Take the flowers from the cauldron and place them in the center. Leave them there.

12

THE WICCANING

The apprentice waits one year and one day,
To take the vows and shed the gray.
Bathed in essence by lighted moon,
Eight candles glow in smoky room.
The journey is long, the road is hard,
Endurance within the soul is carved.
Priestess, Witches, and the Crones
Gather together to cast the stones.
The apprentice calls the Mighty Towers,
And hosts the Deities of the Power.
Before the circle a novice is stripped,
Within the hour, born a Witch.
Adorned with cord and known by name,
Drink the merriment of which is claimed.
Laugh and dance as the music sounds,
Embrace the right to draw the moon down.

BELLADONNA

The Coven

The coven is a group of practicing Witches who work in unison to empower, protect, and help each other and the Universe with works of their magick. The coven contains individuals who practice the same belief system. People in the coven can come from different backgrounds and may not even be close friends, but they have the same beliefs and mutual respect for one another. Every coven has its own set of codes or laws that every member agrees to abide by. All members of the coven have to agree as to what these laws are. This protects the people in the coven and keeps out anyone who could damage the group. The laws work as a positive wall: to protect what is inside and to keep out what is unwanted. Most covens have similar laws. It is important when forming your coven to discuss these laws and for everyone to be in agreement. The ideal size for a coven is from seven to thirteen members. Some covens are very large. A large coven can prohibit the closeness of the group. A coven that is too small may not have enough energy.

When voting on the laws of the coven, the method used is called the Spiral Passage. The Spiral Passage consists of a red mojo and two voting stones, one white or clear, and one black. The white/clear stone is a "yes" and the black stone is a "no." Two different bags or containers are passed during any voting process. The first bag should be an elaborate-looking bag made of velvet. The second bag is to dispose of the second stone. Only the first bag is read when the voting process is done. It is important to have a unanimous decision when voting. This eliminates any potential problems within the coven. Even one opposing vote may cause you to lose some potent coven members over something very trivial. Positive communication and agreements are very important to the backbone of the coven. The voting bags should be present at each and every meeting. When the voting is done, simply retrieve your stones and place them back in your red mojo. The voting stones can be purchased at an occult supply store or you can create your own. Every Witch who is in a coven is required to bring her voting stones to every meeting.

The coven is a base of support for each and every member. If one member is in a crisis, the other members should be there for her or him. The coven can be voted opened or closed to new members. This decision is up to the coven. The coven has to vote on the calendar for each year, such as which Sabbats and which Esbats will be observed. The coven also votes on the position of the acting High Priestess. If a coven has more than one initiated High Priestess, then the group votes as to which responsibilities will fall on each. Another role involved in the coven is a person who will be the Communication Source. This person is responsible for calling all members about any changes in the schedule or program. An appointed High Priestess should be in charge of the coven's Grimoire. This is a collection of spells and rituals that are performed by the group. If there are any initiates for High Priestess, then certain Esbats and Sabbats are assigned to them so they may fulfill the requirements of their initiation. Each member of the coven has a specific responsibility, whether it be preparing food or collecting materials for the spells. A donation is usually required to cover all expenses. It can be a set fee or a total of the expenses divided among everyone. No one should be taken advantage of for expenses; everyone needs to contribute. If a surplus of funds occurs, they are to be used for future events or materials.

The covenstead can rotate or be a set place for each meeting. Again, this is one of the things that needs to be voted on and prearranged. With every vote that the coven places, remember to consider other people's feelings. When selfishness or individual controls enter into the coven, divisiveness can arise among the members. Discuss issues openly and with respect.

All Witches, regardless of whether they participate in covens or are Solitary, are required to obtain a Wiccan name. The Wiccan name is chosen carefully by the individual. The name should be magickal to the Witch and have a specific power or purpose. Some Wiccans keep their Wiccan names for a lifetime, while others may change their names over the years. The reason that Witches may change their names is because they have outgrown them or surpassed the purpose of the names. The members of the coven use the Wiccan names with each other.

Every coven should also have a name. This is voted on by the members and, again, the name should be something very magickal. When large Sabbats are organized and other covens are invited in, it is important for the High Priestess to identify the name of her coven.

When attending a coven meeting, you should always have your voting mojo, your Cord of Measure, your personal talismans and amulets for re-energizing, and your materials for that meeting.

An average coven meeting will last approximately two hours. The first hour is solid ritual work. There should be a Call of Order to every meeting. The rituals should fall in a specific order. If there is a ritual that is to be done for world peace, then this one should go first. The order should follow whatever affects the majority of people first, then move on to what each individual needs. The second hour is to discuss the next meeting and to socialize a bit. This is the time to break out the food and drink. Be considerate of the hostess or host of the covenstead. Do not overstay your welcome. Everyone should adjourn at the same time.

The coven altar should be set and arranged by the hosting member of that covenstead. The altar should be set before the members arrive. The hosting member should perform a ritual cleansing prior to the meeting. The cauldron should be placed somewhere that is accessible to each member. Fire prevention and safety precautions are a must. Some groups have a portable fire extinguisher that is carried from one meeting to another. You have to keep in mind that we have all been burned at the stake once before and prefer not to repeat history by going out in a blaze. All incenses, oils, and other ritual materials should be placed upon the altar before starting.

The common tools for a coven meeting are: incenses and oils, the athame to channel the power, the cauldron, the wand to channel the energy, the chalice, the pentagram, the Unity candle, the Goddess candle, the God candle, the ritual salt and water, the bell, the incense burner, parchment and pens, and any other symbol to represent the meeting or the elements. Whoever is hosting the Covenstead should have these supplies ready and available for the meeting.

When a coven has been practicing for one full year with the same members, then this group will probably exist for a lifetime. If a member does not show up for one-third of the designated meetings, this member is up for review by the coven. This means that if a member does not call in with regrets to the missed meetings and does not actively participate with the other members, then this person may be dismissed from the coven. It is not often that covens dismiss members. Most Witches take their worship seriously; however, in the event that a member does not meet the requirements of the coven laws, then this person is excommunicated from the coven. This process is called Void of Coven.

If a member of a coven decides to go on a spiritual sabbatical for a year or even two, her or his membership in the group is still good and his or her seat is still recognized as filled. This member needs to submit a letter called Coven Retreat that explains why the person will be absent and for how long. This letter should be submitted during a meeting attended by that person.

Every coven should create an initiation ritual for the new members who will come through. This is not a Wiccaning but rather a membership initiation. Most initiations are very simple and offer a warm welcome. If members have to move to a different city or state, their membership may reside with the original coven until another group is started or joined. If Witches are unable to locate a coven, their membership can still be acknowledged with the original coven forever.

Witches can change membership from one coven to another as long as a letter is submitted stating their reason for withdrawal. If a Witch were to denounce her Wiccan rites or to change religions, this needs to be submitted in writing. It is rare, but if a Witch has a change of heart and turns to a dark-hearted person, then the coven has the right to strip that Witch of all his/her white power. This process is called the Darkening. Once a Witch has had the Darkening performed, there is absolutely no return to the coven or to the craft. It is a banishment that lasts for an eternity.

If the world or the nation was in a crisis, such as during a time of war, flood, famine, fire, and so forth, all the covens from around the world would link hands in the sisterhood of Wicca. This means nonstop chant and ritual work to end the crisis. This is why it is important to know what, and how, other covens are working and to keep in touch with them.

If a Witch decides to be a solitary practitioner of the craft, then this person is to be received and respected as much as the next Witch. The Solitary Witch needs to keep updated and informed at all times. The Solitary is responsible for only herself and is not to be convinced or persuaded to join a coven. If the Solitary wants to voluntarily join, then that's fine.

The coven cannot accept any members who are not Witches. This means that if people are sitting on the edge as to what religion they choose, then Wicca is not for them. Witches know that they are Witches just as Catholics know that they are Catholics. People first need to completely go through a Wiccaning before they can join a coven.

Before going through an initiation, a person must have an education in Wicca and be able to answer all the questions. The person needs to know the foundations and rules, and should have practiced this for no less than one year and one day. This individual is considered a Gray Witch until his or her initiation. A Gray Witch must serve in the apprenticeship of a White Witch or High Priestess. During this apprenticeship, the Gray Witch will be challenged and tested by the Goddess and the God. If the Gray Witch does not pass these tests, she or he will not be able to pass initiation. Also, if they do not conquer *purity of heart* within the first six months of their apprenticeship, they are unable to become Witches. The Goddess and the God have an excellent way of working things out.

When preparing for the Wiccaning, a ritual bath must first be taken. During this bath, think about when you decided to become a Witch and what your reasons were. Did your reasons change? Did you change? Think of how you were tested and challenged by the Goddess and God. Think about how you conquered the fears, battles, and problems. Did you earn your right to Wiccaning? Think about what role you can play in a coven or in your practice. What can you do to improve your skills and to become a more effective Witch? These are a few things to ponder. Your ritual bath should be taken in Wiccan bath salts. It also should be taken in the light of eight colored candles. The colors are white, blue, yellow, orange, pink, red, green, and purple. Some occult stores will supply Wiccaning bath salts and oils.

The Wiccaning should not be rehearsed with anyone who is outside of the craft. A fellow Wiccan should help you. The Wiccaning should be planned at least one Moon prior to the event, if not sooner.

You will be asked to perform a spell for the coven. This means you will have to research the day, time, Moon phase, and intention in order to create a spell. Remember, you are actually casting a spell for other Wiccans. Do it right. The Witches who provide your Wiccaning are at your magickal mercy. Research, practice, and memorize your spell.

A coven will provide the initiation, not necessarily an invitation into the coven. Any coven is able to do Wiccanings upon request. This does not mean that the coven wants you to become a member. You can always ask if you can join, but do not be offended or disappointed if a certain coven is closed. The coven can always inform you of any new covens that open, and also keep you on a list so that if any member were to leave you may have the open position.

The High Priestess and the Initiate perform the Wiccaning. The coven members are able to ask specific questions to the Initiate at the appropriate time. It is important to be able to answer the questions as honestly and as in-depth as possible. The Initiate should know how to cast spells and to write her or his own spells. The Initiate needs to know Redes, Sabbats, Moon phases, and so forth. At this time, the Initiate should have had experience in casting, brewing, healing, and divining.

Most Witches start collecting herbs, oils, incenses, wands, oracles, and so forth, early in their education. Many Witches store their supplies in trunks, which can also serve as ready-made altars. Keeping all supplies secret is very important. Keeping the secrets of the trade is essential in working magick. If a Witch were to allow strangers to view the tools, they would need to be consecrated again. It is my opinion that strangers never be allowed to view, touch, or know anything about this religion, unless, of course, they are seriously considering the religion for themselves. Never let people have the opportunity to pass judgment upon you. Keep the Grimoires and all tools sacred and private. Keep your coven protected and private.

Some Decisions for the Coven

1. The name of the coven.
2. The acting High Priestess.
3. Is the coven open or closed to new members? How many members are in this coven?
4. Who will keep the coven Grimoire?
5. Which Sabbats and Esbats will be celebrated as a coven?
6. What are the laws of this coven?
   a. Are any guests allowed to attend? If so, what rules do they abide by? Can they attend more than one meeting?

    b. What is the responsibility of each member? Do you have to attend every single meeting?

    c. Where will the covenstead be?

    d. What happens if a member does not act appropriately and needs to be told so? Who will do this?

    e. What is the cost for each meeting and who will delegate who brings what?

    f. Should the rules of the coven and the positions of the members be voted on every year or are they permanent?

    g. What will be the initiation for new members?

7. What will be the coven's Call of Order?

8. What will be the coven's opening ritual?

9. Will people use their Wiccan names when assembling?

10. What will be the ceremonies used for births, Handfasting, Handparting, passovers, Wiccaning, High Priestesshood, Croning, and so forth?

11. Will there be a designated person for healings, readings, spiritual guidance, astrology, and so forth?

12. What will be the attire of the coven?

13. What if a member does not contribute as much as he or she needs to? Who will be the spokesperson to tell this member?

14. Will there be an energy-raising to start the meeting? Who will conduct this?

15. What is the exact Call of Order for the Sabbats?

16. What is the exact Call of Order for the Esbats?

17. What is the length of time for each meeting?

18. Who will write or research the spells for the coven?

19. If there are excess funds in the coven, where will they go and who will oversee them?

20. Who will be the Communication Source and will this job rotate?

21. Who will record the Spiral Passage and make sure that everyone has a list of the Laws?
22. Will Solitaries be allowed to join the coven?
23. Who will prepare the altar and materials for each meeting?
24. Will the coven invest in coven tools?
25. What are the reasons for immediate dismissal from the coven?

The Darkening

TOOLS Three black candles, Widdershins incense and oil, black cord, a poppet, a photograph or hair and nails to identify this person, belladonna, thirteen straight pins, a red mojo, black electrical tape, and a box that is shaped like a coffin.

INSTRUCTIONS Light the black candles and the incense. Create a poppet for the intended. In the red mojo, place the hair and nails or the photograph of the intended along with belladonna. Anoint the mojo with Widdershins oil. Place the mojo in the head of the poppet. Make the poppet look like the intended, with any extra detail that would make this look more real. With the black electrical tape, bind the poppet starting at the feet and moving upward to the head. Make the poppet resemble a black mummy. With the black cord, tie a noose around the neck of the poppet. With the thirteen pins, pierce the seven major chakras plus one in each hand and foot and one in each ear. Place the poppet in the coffin and seal it shut permanently. On the outside of the coffin write the Wiccan name of the intended and bury it outside, away from your home.

INCANTATION

> The day of endings now in wane,
> For the Witch who knows no shame.
> The day of darkening has now come,
> Your days of Witchery are all done.
> No longer held in mind or heart,
> Your white and purity has grown dark.

Bound by darkness and smoked in reverse,
What once was a gift is now your curse.
Three black flames upward burn,
Unlocking the magick that you've learned.
The memory weakens, but the Witches know,
Your third eye shuts and forever is closed.
The head is filled with deadly nightshade,
To reclaim the powers of weavings you made.
Anointed and pinned in the thirteen hearts,
To deaden the magick in which you part.
The noose in place will tighten and choke,
If ever you wear the Witch's cloak.
The coven has voted and you have lost,
Your Wiccan rite will pay the cost.
No longer family to the Witch,
Your fate is sealed, black as pitch.
In the tomb of forgotten hearts,
Alone and helpless, in the dark.
So Mote It Be.

Remember that *only* when the Witch has turned completely black and it is voted unanimously by the coven to release this member can this spell be performed. It is highly recommended that twelve moons pass before acting upon this spell. If the Witch has not had a change of heart before that time, then the spell is cast. Avoid hasty decisions and try to help the stray Witch. If the Witch turns to black that easily, then he or she was probably never a true Witch from the beginning and the power stripping should go smoothly and easily.

The Wiccaning

The Wiccaning is the initiation rite to become a Witch. The Wiccaning should be scheduled during a High Sabbat. This is not a hard and fast rule, but rather a tradition. A Wiccaning may take place during any waxing phase of the Moon. Some Wiccanings are combined with a coven initiation. If a Witch chooses to be a Solitary, a High Priestess and a coven should still perform the Wiccaning. A solitary Witch still needs to perform before peers. Because this is such a special ceremony, a lot of preparation is needed.

The Initiate needs to be able to perform an energy raising and have a spell prepared to cast. The Initiate needs to be rehearsed on the exact procedure of the ritual and also know how to answer the basic questions. The Initiate is responsible for bringing the wine for toasting and food for the celebration afterward. The altar needs to be set before anyone arrives. The Initiate needs to bring the Cord of Measure and to be wearing the appropriate attire.

This is a high ceremony. It is a time of personal dedication to the Goddess and the God. The ritual bath is the final step before your life will change. Relax. Meditate. Open your heart to the Universal Power and let your light shine. Contemplate the role you are about to take and the possible changes it will have in your life.

The Initiation Rite to Become a Witch

Set your altar prior to the initiation rite.

1. Seat your elders. When ready to begin, cleanse the circle. (A full ceremony requires sweeping and then the salt and water cleansing ritual.)

2. Cast your circle and alert the circle.

3. Invoke the Spirits and call the Quadrants.

4. Invoke the Goddess and God.

5. The High Priestess states the purpose.

6. Energy raising.

7. Draw down the Moon.

8. Test the power.

9. Take the vows.

10. Spiral Passage

11. Receive the cord.

12. The toast and High Priestess's blessing are performed.

13. Adjourn the Spirits, dismiss the Quadrants, and show grati-
    tude to the Goddess and God. Open the circle.

To CLEANSE THE CIRCLE   Sweep the outer perimeter of the circle.
Place three pinches of salt into the bowl of water. Recite:

> I cleanse thee Spirit of salt and Spirit of water. I cast out all
> impurities that lie within thee. It is my will, So Mote It Be.

Sprinkle the outside of the circle in deosil motion.

> This circle is now clean.

CAST THE CIRCLE   Recite:

> Blessed be sunrise, sunset, midnight, and noon,
> When two or more shall gather to draw down the moon.

ALERT THE CIRCLE   Kneel before the altar. Ring the ceremonial
bell. Recite:

> I conjure thee, O' Circle of Truth.
> Encompass the powers of heaven and earth.
> Combine the energies within this magick circle.
> I stand before this circle as a Gray novice.
> My intention is to be recognized as a White Witch.
> I pray that I am worthy.
> This is my will, So Mote It Be.

CALL THE QUADRANTS   With the athame, draw the sign of the pentagram in the air (use the invoking method). Begin by facing the
East.

> Raphael!
> I call upon the Powers of the East.
> May the Air lift me so my mind will feast.
> Michael!
> I call upon the Powers of the South.
> May the Fire of free will never burn out.
> Gabriel!

234

I call upon the Powers of the West.
May the Water of emotion join my quest.
Uriel!
I call upon the Powers of the North.
May the Earth be my body from this day forth.
So Mote It Be.

INVOKE THE GOD AND GODDESS   Kneel before the altar. Light the God and Goddess candles. Raise your arms upward. Recite:

Lord of Light, Creator of Man.
I welcome Thee to empower this magick circle.
Lady of Light, Creator of Woman.
I welcome Thee to empower this magick circle.

The Initiate now faces the coven and says:

I welcome all of you here.

STATE THE PURPOSE (DONE BY THE HIGH PRIESTESS)   High Priestess:

We are gathered here within this Circle of Truth in unison with the Goddess and God and the Guardian Angels and Their Towers. Our purpose for this magick circle is to acknowledge the Wiccaning of our new sister (brother). We have watched (first name) *grow from a novice of Gray to a blossoming White Witch. I pray to our governing hosts that she (he) is worthy. The remaining power of this ceremony is to be performed by* (Wiccan name), *our new sister (brother).*

ENERGY RAISING   The Initiate now leads in a chant or song to raise the energy.

DRAW DOWN THE MOON   The Initiate has created a very special spell for this Wiccaning. The spell is to be cast before all who are gathered. It is important to memorize the spell and to cast it with confidence.

TEST THE POWER   The Initiate now stands at the head of the circle. The High Priestess is directly across from the Initiate. The Initiate

says, "I am now ready for the test." All of the questions are asked by
the High Priestess and the Initiate answers all of the questions.

HIGH PRIESTESS: How long have you served in your
apprenticeship?
INITIATE: No less than one year and one day.
HIGH PRIESTESS: State the Quadrants, their Guardians, their
element, and their purpose.
INITIATE: Raphael—Guardian of the East. This is Air. This is
my mind. Michael—Guardian of the South. This is Fire. This
is my free will. Gabriel—Guardian of the West. This is Water.
This is my emotions. Uriel—Guardian of the North. This is
Earth. This is my body.
HIGH PRIESTESS: Who are the Triple Goddess and Triple God
and what do they mean to you?
INITIATE: The Goddess is: the Maiden, the Mother, and the
Crone. The God is: the Father, the Son, and the Holy Spirit.
These are the Almighty Powers that be. This is Whom I
worship.
HIGH PRIESTESS: Name the seven laws of magick.

INITIATE:

1. Balance

2. Maturity

3. Compassion

4. Wisdom

5. Self-Discipline

6. Perseverance

7. Devotion

HIGH PRIESTESS: Name all of the Sabbats.
INITIATE: The High Sabbats are Beltane, Lammas, Samhain,
and Candlemas. The Lower Sabbats are Ostara, Litha,
Mabon, and Yule.
HIGH PRIESTESS: You have set your altar with thirteen tools.
Name the tools and their purpose.

INITIATE:

1. (Large Candle) This is the Unity of power.

2. (White Candle to the Left) This represents the God.

3. (White Candle to the Right) This represents the Goddess.

4. This is the incense to attract the Power.

5. This is the chalice to toast the Power.

6. This is the athame to draw the Energy.

7. This is the wand to channel the Energy.

8. This is my oracle in which I divine.

9. This is the oil for anointing.

10. This is the pentagram. Its five points represent Earth, Air, Fire, Water, and the Spirit.

11. This is the bell to alert the circle.

12. This is the ritual salt.

13. This is the water that combines with the salt to make the holy water of consecration.

HIGH PRIESTESS: For what purpose have you selected this religion?

INITIATE: To aid my brothers and sisters in their efforts to benefit the world and the Universe.

HIGH PRIESTESS: What is the Wiccan Rede?

INITIATE: An harm ye none, then do as ye will.

HIGH PRIESTESS: What do you have to offer?

INITIATE: I have purity of heart.

TAKE THE VOWS

HIGH PRIESTESS: You stand at the threshold of Heaven and Earth. How do you come to this circle?

INITIATE: With perfect love and perfect trust.

HIGH PRIESTESS: To what name do you choose to be known to the Goddess and the God and among your pagan siblings?

INITIATE: _____ (This is your Wiccan name.)

HIGH PRIESTESS: (Wiccan name), do you swear to keep the

secrets of the Wiccan tradition and all of the secrets that
have been revealed to you?

INITIATE: Yes.

HIGH PRIESTESS: Do you promise to honor and defend your
belief and to assist any of your pagan siblings in this task?

INITIATE: Yes.

HIGH PRIESTESS: At this time, do you choose a coven and a
covenstead?

INITIATE: (If the answer is yes, then name the coven) (if the
answer is no, then state that you wish to be a solitary
practitioner).

SPIRAL PASSAGE   The coven members will now vote whether the
Initiate has passed the Wiccaning. If a coven has been chosen, the
members will cast the stones for a second Spiral Passage for acceptance into the coven. If the Witch declares to be in a solitary practice, then simply move on to the Cord of Measure.

RECEIVE THE CORD

HIGH PRIESTESS:

(Hold cord to the height of the Initiate.)
With this measure and then plus one,
Your days of weaving have now begun.
Round and round from night to noon,
You have received your power, draw down the Moon . . .
So Mote It Be!!!

TOAST AND BLESSING   The new Witch hands the High Priestess
the anointing oil. The High Priestess says:

You have now proven your knowledge, your power, and your
devotion. In the name of the Holy Trinity of the Goddess and the
God, I now present to this magick circle, (new Wiccan name,) a
White Witch.

The new Witch pours wine into everyone's cup. The person to the
right of the new Witch starts with a blessing for her or him. It continues in deosil motion and ends with the High Priestess. (No one

drinks until the High Priestess ends the toast.) At the end of the toast, all raise their chalices and say:

So Mote It Be.

All drink.

ADJOURNING PROCEDURE   The new Witch now starts the adjournment of the magick circle.

Dismiss the Quadrants: Face West and using the athame, draw the pentagram in the air (use the releasing method.) Recite:

To the North, South, East, and West, I dismiss with gratitude and so be blessed.

Adjourn the Spirits:

To the Angels and Spirits that guard the Towers, with gratitude in aiding this magickal hour.

Thanks to Goddess and God:

To the mighty Goddess and God that be, with gratitude and praise, So Mote It Be.

OPEN THE CIRCLE   The new Witch snuffs out the candles of the Goddess and God. The Unity candle is to be held with two hands while saying:

This candle now shines of one.
My journey has now begun.
This circle is now open,
But is forever unbroken.
So Mote It Be.

Snuff out the candle.
Adjourn to the festivities!

Rite to Power

The Rite to Power is the initiation to Priestess or Priesthood. This is the time in midlife when the initiated Witch has been in practice for a minimum of two to three years. In the old practice of the religion, midlife was considered to be about thirty-six years old. It is usually after your child-birthing time has waned and your empowerment as a Witch has grown significantly.

The Rite to Power is *not* a ritual to receive more power. It is rather a time to share the power and knowledge you have and to offer your services to your coven and to help those in need. It is a manifestation of a very comfortable feeling about life and where you are in life.

Even if a Witch is Solitary, the Rite to Power should be considered. The commitment is to help the world in making positive changes and to aid any Witches in whatever difficult times they may have. The time of Priestess or Priesthood is approximately eighteen to twenty-five years long. The time of a Crone is after this phase. The Rite to Power honors the Goddess in the second phase of your life.

This ritual is a high ceremony. A ritual bath with three white candles and Wiccan bath salts is taken before the ceremony begins. It is a serious and beautiful ceremony that is relaxed and serene. A white or white and gold Cingula is necessary for the Initiate to have ready and be placed upon the altar.

The Ceremony

The Initiate needs to send out invitations to the coven. The Initiate also supplies the entire feast after the ceremony. The Initiate seats all coven members and has rehearsed the ceremony with the acting High Priestess. The preparation for this rite is no less than three Full Moons.

1. Sweep the circle.
2. Cleanse the circle.
3. Cast the circle.
4. Alert the circle: (Kneel before the altar. Ring the bell.)

Recite:

> *I conjure Thee, O' Circle of Truth.*
> *Encompass the powers of Heaven and Earth.*
> *Combine these energies within this magick circle.*
> *I stand before this Circle as a White Witch.*
> *My intention is to be recognized as a High Priestess (Priest).*
> *I pray that I am worthy.*
> *This is my will, So Mote It Be.*

5. Invoke the Quadrants.
6. Invoke the Goddess and the God.

INITIATE: I am ready for the test.

HIGH PRIESTESS: You stand at the threshold of Heaven and Earth. How do you come to this magick circle?

INITIATE: With perfect love and perfect trust.

HIGH PRIESTESS: What do you have to offer?

INITIATE: I have purity of heart.

HIGH PRIESTESS: At this time, do you wish to change your Wiccan name or do you prefer to be initiated as (current Wiccan name)?

INITIATE: I wish to be presented as _____.

HIGH PRIESTESS: How do you represent the Goddess?

INITIATE: I symbolize the Goddess in the second phase. I have vitality, knowledge, and the gift of sharing. I wish to serve the Goddess in this light.

HIGH PRIESTESS: I draw the star of magick upon your power. (Anoint the third eye area with Power oil and make the sign of the pentagram.)

INITIATE: I thank you, High Priestess. I will do my best to see through the eyes of the Goddess, to hear with the ears of the Goddess, and to speak with the wisdom of the Goddess.

HIGH PRIESTESS: At this time, (Initiate) will perform her (his) magick of the Power of Wisdom.

The Initiate must perform an elaborate spell. It may include dancing, singing, drumming, and so forth. It is to be dramatic, original, and effective. The spell's theme is wisdom. After this casting, the Initiate will break bread with the coven. She will offer a loaf of bread of which every member receives a slice. She will then pour red wine into all chalices. At that point she says:

> *I offer the Goddess, the assistance of my body. I offer the Goddess, the assistance of my blood—my life force. Please join me in this dedication.*

(All eat of the bread and wine.)

SPIRAL PASSAGE

HIGH PRIESTESS: You have been voted in favor of your High Priestess/Priesthood. Stand to receive your Cord of Power.

HIGH PRIESTESS: With this Cord, I surround you with light, love, and power. Welcome High Priestess/Priest, for we honor and value your presence.

All coven members toast a specific blessing that will aid the new High Priestess or Priest in her or his endeavors, ending with the High Priestess (no one drinks until the High Priestess ends the toast).

The new High Priestess or Priest will now:

Dismiss the Quadrants.
Adjourn the Angels and Good Spirits.
Thank the Goddess and the God.
Open the Circle.

Adjourn to the festivities!

Rite to Crowning

Croning and Elderhood are rites performed when Wiccans have reached a certain age in wisdom. In years past, Croning and Elderhood were received at age fifty-six. This is when women have stopped their menstrual cycle and men have decreased in their physical strength. This is regarded as the third phase of life. At this point in the Wiccan religion, the Witch must have completed the Wiccaning and High Priestess or Priesthood. The next phase is to Crone.

The passage into Croning and Elderhood means to enter into the wise age.

In light of the neopagan attitude, Croning may occur at other times than at the age of fifty-six. The main reason the age of fifty-six was chosen is that the planet Saturn will have returned to its original point in the natal chart twice.

The Rite to Crown is a beautiful and festive ceremony. The acting High Priestess performs it. The entire coven is responsible for the activities, food and drink, and the gift that is to be given to the Crone.

The Ceremony

The altar is set with the usual tools and decorated with fresh flowers. A special gift is to be placed upon the altar for the person who is Croning. One of the coven members is in charge of sending invitations to the other members. It is not a surprise to the person who is Croning that this ceremony is occurring. Full ritual wardrobe is required. This is to be performed on an evening during the Hare Moon.

A coven member will cleanse the circle.

The High Priestess will cast the circle:

> Round and round the Moon has shown,
> Empower us now with the Rite to Crone.

She then rings the bell.

A coven member will invoke the Quadrants:

> Watch Towers of the East . . . Raphael! We summon thee.
> Watch Towers of the South . . . Michael! We summon thee.
> Watch Towers of the West . . . Gabriel! We summon thee.
> Watch Towers of the North . . . Uriel! We summon thee.

The High Priestess invokes the Goddess and God:

> Lord of Life, we see Your Light,
> Come to us this Crowning night.
> Lady of Love, we feel Your presence,

Bless us with Your holy essence.
So Mote It Be.

The High Priestess states the purpose:

We gather here to celebrate our sister (brother) _____
(Wiccan name) who has come into the wise age. This is her (his)
Rite to Crown. The person who stands before you has grown from
a novice to an elder with knowledge. Her (his) wisdom of the
heart will benefit each one of us. This is now our elder sister
(brother) whom we greatly respect.

Representing the Goddess in the third phase, the Lady of
Unlimited Power, you are now honored in Her likeness. We offer
you our respect and love from now until eternity.

The circle now stands with the Crone in the center. The Crone rings
the bell for each year of her life. While the bell is ringing, the coven
chants a special prayer. At the end of the ringing, the Crone stands
and the coven sits down.

The Crone says:

I have chosen a special Witch to share my wisdom with. (The
selected coven member stands beside her.) *This is (Wiccan*
name) *whom I have selected to give this heirloom* (a piece of
jewelry that has a purple stone in it). *This is to remind you that*
I will be in your heart for eternity. I will always be your teacher
and friend. I will give you aid from this world and into the next.

The coven says:

So Mote It Be.

The High Priestess now stands beside the Crone to present the Cord
of Crowning. As she ties the Cord around her (him), she recites:

Lord and Lady bless this Crown,
Bless our elder with favor.
Bless the wisdom in her (his) heart,
For all of us to savor.
So Mote It Be.

The High Priestess presents the Crone with a special gift that is magickal and very precious. She says:

> We present this magickal gift to our Crone. May it always bring you happiness and good health.

All the members of the coven toast the Crone, ending with the High Priestess.

A coven member will dismiss the Quadrants:

> To the North, South, East, and West,
> With gratitude and praise, so be blessed.

The High Priestess thanks the Goddess and God:

> Lord and Lady of Infinite Power,
> We thank Thee for this magickal hour.

The Crone opens the circle:

> This candle now shines of one,
> Our journey has now begun.
> This circle is now open,
> But is forever unbroken.
> So Mote It Be.

Adjourn to the festivities!

Final Thoughts

The path to becoming a Witch is not a simple one. In fact, the first year when you are a Gray Witch will be the hardest year of your life. Do not hurry your process, but accept the challenges facing you. Always reflect back to the ten basic rules. They will give you the structure you need. I have witnessed dozens of individuals get to the final phase of their one-year initiation and abandon ship. The reasons all varied. The strength you will need comes only from you, not the Goddess and God. Remember, this is *Their* test for you. If you are dedicated and strong enough to endure the first year, the rest is easy.

The following are the basics of Wicca. Different sects will vary, but the worship of the Goddess and God is consistent. Never be persuaded into believing anything your heart does not agree with. You be the judge. Take control of your own life. Be true to yourself, and harm none.

If for any reason you are unable to locate a practicing coven in your area and you are ready to be Wiccaned, do not despair. I can help you complete your Wiccaning. I have been a High Priestess for many years and am looking forward to my Croning. You can write to me for instructions (please enclose a S.A.S.E.) and I will send you the information you need to do your Wiccaning by mail. If you need a good occult store, I can include information on how to get in touch with the store I purchase my supplies from.

I wish you a lifetime of success and spiritual perfection. Blessed Be!

Sister Moon
P.O. Box 2995
Loveland, CO 80539
sismoon0101@aol.com

13

THE SPELLS

Keep in mind what they say,
About those Witches and their ways.
The Witch's familiar rings the bell,
Whenever the hag casts her spell.
Cackle and giggle, hiss and bite,
At the garden in full moon light.
Watch that Witch fly her broom,
Preying upon an open tomb.
Searching for souls to pawn and sell,
Making deals created in hell.
Beware the recipes within the book,
The Witch will brew, burn, and cook.
Guard your children and your pets,
For these will make her appetite whet.
Refuse to look a Witch's way,
Or she will think you want to play.
Close your mind and your heart,
Keep your fear safe in the dark.

BELLADONNA

Blanching the Heart (White)

MAGICKAL INTENTION   To have purity of heart.

TIME   Waning Friday, Venus hour.

TOOLS   One large white candle, one small votive candle, Aura Cleansing incense, Purity oil, salt, water, and any type of rose oil. You will also need to find a beautiful place in nature that has a swift-moving stream or body of water.

INSTRUCTIONS   Anoint both white candles with Purity oil. Light both candles and the Aura Cleansing incense. The small votive candle represents yourself. The large white candle represents the person you are going to become. Create the holy water of consecration: Add three pinches of salt to clean water and recite:

> *I cleanse thee Spirit of Salt and Spirit of Water. I cast out all impurities that lie within thee. This is my will, So Mote It Be.*

Add one drop of Rose oil to the consecrated water. Find a place on the ground that is touched by the sun and not terribly crowded by the trees. Position yourself so that the body of water is to the west of you. Anoint yourself with the holy water of consecration. Call upon the Goddess in a loud and clear voice, asking to receive purity of heart. Tell the Goddess you are completely prepared to receive this gift and you are willing to be improved by Her guidance. When you feel Her presence, allow the energy to flow up from the earth, into your body, and out through the top of your head. Recite the incantation. When you feel the physical and emotional change, return to your home. You will know you have been successful when you no longer experience hate, grievance, intolerance, self-pity, or jealousy. It is quite normal to return home and sleep for several hours. Upon awakening, you will feel refreshed and vibrant. If for any reason you do not feel significant changes about yourself or others, then wait three months and cast the spell again.

The Goddess delivers perfection with purity of heart. The changes within you will be obvious, unless, of course, you already have a pure heart. Purity will then be abundant in all that you do. Within thirty days you shall have at least two different people remark about how different you seem, or compliment you on how you have improved. Have total assurance that your spell has been granted. If after three castings of this spell there are no changes, then place your efforts into cleansings and the repelling of negative energies until purity of heart can be achieved.

INCANTATION

> *Goddess of Heart, Goddess of Soul,*
> *Blanch my heart and make me whole.*
> *No pain of wrongdoings shall cross my days,*
> *I give you my heart to cleanse your way.*
> *I remain in test for one Moon term,*
> *Hoping to receive what I need to learn.*
> *Blanch my heart and keep me pure,*
> *Take the darkness as I receive the cure.*
> *Open my eyes and let me see,*
> *All the beauty you gave to me.*
> *So Mote It Be.*

The Crystal Healing (Yellow)

MAGICKAL INTENTION   To manifest healing by way of transference.

TIME   Waning Monday, Sun Hour.

TOOLS   Three yellow candles, Healing incense, High Meadows oil, a crystal bowl with clean water, horehound herb, a sliced clove of garlic, one quartz crystal, one eucalyptus leaf, and one salmon-colored cloth to be placed beneath the crystal bowl.

INSTRUCTIONS   Anoint the candles with High Meadows oil. Place all ingredients in the room where the sick person is lying. Light the candles and the incense. Place a small table near the sick person and cover it with the salmon-colored cloth. Place the crystal bowl with water, the clove of garlic, the horehound, the quartz crystal, and the eucalyptus leaf on top of the table. The spell works by absorbing the sickness through the garlic and releasing the healing energy through the horehound. The quartz crystal is the conductor and the eucalyptus is the spark. Recite the incantation. You may repeat this spell three times within a thirty-six-hour period. Bury the herbs and the water away from your home. The candles, oil, incense, quartz crystal, crystal bowl, and the cloth may all be reused.

INCANTATION

> *Horehound herb be near the sick,*
> *Release, absorb, bury the quick.*
> *Moon day high within the sun,*
> *Release, absorb, illness be done.*
> *Carry disease to garlic clove,*
> *Release, absorb, recovery be wove.*
> *Crystal healing in crystal shell,*
> *Release, absorb, all be well.*
> *So Mote It Be.*

Angel's Wings (Blue)

MAGICKAL INTENTION   To promote protection from slander, hate, and all negative energies.

TIME   Hare Moon, Mercury hour.

TOOLS   One blue candle, Protection incense, Jinx Removing oil or Protection oil.

INSTRUCTIONS   Anoint the candle with the oil. Light the candle and the incense. Visualize yourself with a bright blue aura. Recite the incantation. From this time until the next Hare Moon, if you feel any negative energy coming from someone or something, relight the candle and the incense. This will deter all negativity from coming near you.

INCANTATION

> Guardian Angels with pale blue wings,
> Wrap me within the love you bring.
> Shelter me from the thunder and storm,
> Flutter the wings that keep me warm.
> Protect me from the negative ones,
> That judge me with their slandering tongues.
> Protect me from evil and the hate,
> And all the energies they precipitate.
> Replace the darkness by protecting me,
> This is my will, So Mote It Be.

To Snare a Snake (Pink)

MAGICKAL INTENTION   To make someone fall in love with you.

TIME   Full Moon, Venus hour.

TOOLS   One pink candle, Lovers incense, Cupid oil, seven beans, one black snakeroot herb, and a twenty-four-inch piece of pink yarn.

INSTRUCTIONS   Anoint the candle with Cupid oil. Light the candle and the incense. Visualize this specific individual greeting you at your front door. Visualize his or her smile and the look of love in his or her eyes. Make a circle with the pink yarn. Place the circle under the doormat of your home. Place the seven beans around the inside of the yarn and the black snakeroot in the center of the circle. After everything is in place, recite the incantation. Light the pink candle at least once a day until the intended has come your way. The individual must walk across or stand upon the circle within twenty-eight days of casting this spell. The person must do this without any knowledge of what he or she is crossing.

INCANTATION

> Circle pink under rounded moon,
> Sings to lovers a magickal tune.
> Seven beans to lure and attract,
> One herb of snake, rigid, and black.
> Love is the potion, love is the cure,
> Love be mine, perfect and pure.
> Come into my garden and into the snare,
> Your love is waiting to find you there.
> So Mote It Be.

Passion Potion (Red)

MAGICKAL INTENTION   To arouse passion.

TIME   Full Moon, Venus hour.

TOOLS   Two red candles, Flaming Heart incense, Passion oil, whiskey, Seven-Up, a dash of ginseng, a dash of musk, and a dash of cornsilk.

INSTRUCTIONS   Anoint the red candles with Passion oil. Light the candles and the incense. Make this brew outside: combine whiskey, Seven-Up, ginseng, musk, and cornsilk. Recite the incantation and suffumigate the brew with the incense. Serve over ice and enjoy.

INCANTATION

> Rounded moon and passions flow,
> Into this brew it must go.
> Touch my man and warm his groin,
> Make him tremor when we do join.
> Alay. Kaseacz. Into my brew!
> Power and energy and lusting, too.
> Hard and rising when he drinks of thee,
> Also whenever he thinks of me.
> So Mote It Be.

Skull in the Pocket (Orange)

MAGICKAL INTENTION   To make yourself irresistible to others, whether it is for love, business, or attention.

TIME   Hare Moon, Moon hour.

TOOLS   One orange candle, Drawing incense, VooDoo Night oil, one red mojo, scullcap herb, one vanilla bean, and one horseshoe magnet.

INSTRUCTIONS   Anoint the candle with VooDoo Night oil. Light the candle and the incense. Visualize yourself looking more radiant and beautiful than ever. See yourself smiling and laughing. Place the scullcap, the vanilla bean, and the magnet in the red mojo. Suffumigate the mojo in deosil motion while reciting the incantation. Carry the mojo with you at all times. Place the mojo in full moonlight to recharge.

INCANTATION

> *Dark of moon and power of skull,*
> *Make me shine and never dull.*
> *Attract to me the light I need,*
> *Recognition completes the deed.*
> *I carry the skull, bean, and shoe,*
> *Clockwise smoked with Night VooDoo.*
> *Somber all others so my eminence shines,*
> *Attract, compel, and make me divine.*
> *So Mote It Be.*

Dead Man's Mojo (Green)

MAGICKAL INTENTION   To attract money and financial success.

TIME   Full Moon, Jupiter hour.

TOOLS   One green candle, Helping Hand incense, Money Drawing oil, red mojo, one tonka wishing bean, and moss from a gravestone.

INSTRUCTIONS   Anoint the candle with Money Drawing oil. Light the candle and incense. Obtain some moss growing on a gravestone. If the dead person was wealthy, all the better. Place the moss in the red mojo along with the tonka bean. Suffumigate the mojo in deosil motion. Recite the incantation. Keep the mojo in your pocket to attract money. This spell works best if the mojo is worn against the body.

INCANTATION

Headstone, headstone, dead man's purse,
Bring me money, wealth, and worth.
Luck be with me, silver be cold,
Cash abundant, surround by gold.
So Mote It Be.

Smoking Spirits (Purple)

MAGICKAL INTENTION   To strengthen psychic powers when seeking guidance.

TIME   Hare Moon, Mercury hour.

TOOLS   One purple candle, Moon incense, Psychic oil, tobacco, wormwood, thistle, and dandelion herbs.

INSTRUCTIONS   Anoint the candle with Psychic oil and light it. Combine the herbs into the incense, or even roll the herbs into a cigarette and ignite the incense separately. The idea is to inhale the smoke of the herbs. Recite the incantation and then ask your questions. The answers will soon come to you.

INCANTATION

I call upon the Spirit Wise,
To reveal the answers and open my eyes.
Speak to me as I invoke,
Truth and wisdom through this smoke.
I honor your presence with these herbs,
I anxiously await your every word.

Candle burns with violet fire,
Truth be told from Spirits higher.
So Mote It Be.

The Wedding Bell (Brown)

MAGICKAL INTENTION   To make your marriage happen sooner.

TIME   Hare Moon, Mercury hour.

TOOLS   A pink candle, Lover's incense, Cedarwood oil, a bell, and a red mojo. Also, you will need material to make a love poppet of your betrothed (it should be skin-colored material), hair and nails from your lover, jasmine, dill, bloodroot, mandrake, and witch grass.

INSTRUCTIONS   Place in the red mojo healthy pinches of jasmine, dill, bloodroot, mandrake, witch grass, and the hair and nails from your lover. Make the poppet to resemble your lover. Stuff with a batting-type material so that the poppet is well filled out. Place the red mojo in the heart of the poppet. Place the remaining amounts of jasmine, dill, bloodroot, mandrake, and witch grass in a bath. Once they are in the bath, light the pink candle. Place Cedarwood oil in the water and burn the Lover's incense while bathing. Suffumigate the poppet with the burning incense and anoint the doll with the bath water. Ring the bell. When the bath is done, recite the incantation and place the poppet under your pillow. When the proposal comes, take the poppet to fast-flowing water and throw it in. If another person finds it in the water, it will bring love to their life.

INCANTATION

I have bathed my love in the half of the Moon,
Let the proposal of marriage come to me soon.
The glorious chime begins this spell,
The poppet's heart will never tell.
Carry my love all the way,
Carry me to our wedding day.
My husband calls from the days ahead,

Tucked in safely from my bed.
Hear the chant, I've cast the spell,
Hear the chime of our wedding bell.
So Mote It Be.

A Thorn in the Side (Gray)

MAGICKAL INTENTION   To repel a specific person from you.

TIME   Waning Saturday, Moon hour.

TOOLS   One gray candle, JuJu incense, Widdershins oil, thistle, thorns from a white rose, sagebrush, pine needles, nettle, a picture of the person you want to repel, and one red mojo.

INSTRUCTIONS   Anoint the candle with Widdershins oil. Light the candle and the incense. Place the picture of the person you want to repel into the red mojo along with the thistle, thorns, sagebrush, pine needles, and nettle. Suffumigate over the incense in a widdershins motion. Bury the mojo in an area beside a cemetery. Recite the incantation over the mojo before you bury it.

INCANTATION

Repelling Spirits discharge and decay,
Take _____ far away.
Counter-clockwise churn and burn,
Make _____ about-face turn.
Distant from me and thoughts erased,
Put flowers and gardens in my place.
If will be strong and my wish denied,
Place a thorn in _____'s side.
Prod and poke to inspire the pain,
Till the obsession begins to wane.
For every thought that has action or deed,
The thorn will pierce and make him bleed.
So Mote It Be.